THE OTHER SIDE OF HISTORY

a unique view
of momentous
events from the
last 60 years

SIMON MAIER

D1662380

Marshall Cavendish
Editions

Published by Marshall Cavendish Editions
An imprint of Marshall Cavendish International

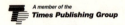

A member of the
Times Publishing Group

Other Marshall Cavendish Offices:
Marshall Cavendish Corporation. 99 White Plains Road, Tarrytown NY 10591-9001, USA • Marshall Cavendish International (Thailand) Co Ltd. 253 Asoke, 12th Flr, Sukhumvit 21 Road, Klongtoey Nua, Wattana, Bangkok 10110, Thailand • Marshall Cavendish (Malaysia) Sdn Bhd, Times Subang, Lot 46, Subang Hi-Tech Industrial Park, Batu Tiga, 40000 Shah Alam, Selangor Darul Ehsan, Malaysia

Marshall Cavendish is a registered trademark of Times Publishing Limited

National Library Board, Singapore Cataloguing-in-Publication Data

Name(s): Maier, Simon. | Marshall Cavendish Editions, publisher.
Title: The other side of history : a unique view of momentous events from the last 60 years / Simon Maier.
Description: Singapore : Marshall Cavendish Edition, [2017]
Identifier(s): OCN 978256100 | ISBN 978-981-4771-37-5 (paperback)
Subject(s): LCSH: History, Modern--20th century--Anecdotes. | History, Modern--21st century--Anecdotes.
Classification: DDC 909.82--dc23

Printed in Singapore by Markono Print Media Pte Ltd

This book is for my brother, Michael.

"All the world's a stage,

And all the men and women merely players;

They have their exits and their entrances,

And one man in his time plays many parts, ..."

From *As You Like It*, Act II, Scene VII,
William Shakespeare

CONTENT

A NOTE

Subject: Thank you!

Hi Sarah,

Just got back to London from NY via a few days in Venice (my favourite city) and I wanted to drop you a quick mail to thank you very much for helping make my visit to the New York office so enjoyable. Obviously I had a great time with my grandfather and he always speaks volumes about you. I was really touched and the food — so much! And all delicious. Thanks too for sorting out flights and everything else. Really appreciated.

I also wanted to thank you for sending the notes that Gramps had given me which I'd left behind — always doing that — plus the photographs. The package beat me home. He's very lucky to have you as a PA! But I think he knows that.

Not sure if I mentioned this to you — or if he did, but I said to him that I'd like to make what he told me into a book. If I can. I think I told you that I've been writing a fair bit for several magazines now, as well as some websites, and that's all going very well. The stuff that he talked about — where he'd been in the world over the last sixty years, what he'd seen, the history that he'd witnessed — all the moments in his life when he'd been part of (or had been close to) events that have made it into the news and the history books. His memory was super good when we talked and, even though he referred to his notebooks and his photos, he was razor-sharp and could recall whole chunks of stuff.

He told me about lots of famous and less famous people. He's always been fascinated by what people do and the kindnesses that they afford him and others. And then he's shocked to the core by the horrors that people can perpetrate and the terrible things those people do in their thirst for power or wealth, or because of hate or prejudice.

You know that his stories are amazing and I know he talks to you about these things. So, once I've written something I'd be really pleased if you'd read it through.

I've got some meetings with people in a couple of months in NY and I'll be staying for around a week, so I'll let Gramps and you know as soon as I've got dates.

See you very soon Sarah and, again, thanks. I had a wonderful afternoon and that was in part down to you.

Best

THE START

Hello, hello! Come in... Thank you, Sarah. Of course you remember Sarah? Sure, you do. Come in, come in. So good to see you. Well, now, it *has* been some time! Of course it has... yes, far too long. Come... Sit down... Yes, absolutely. Sarah, no more calls for a while please... thank you. Yes, yes... of course I won't forget... you'll let us know when the car's here.

Goodness me. A very long time. You've grown, but then grandparents always say that I suppose... You know, time isn't a straight line from A to Z. It curves, it goes down cul-de-sacs. It takes us in many directions. Where opportunity ventures, we must grab it. Sometimes it will be the wrong way — and sometimes the decision will be right in every sense — and the results can be truly wonderful.

It *is* good to see you. So good... Of course, of course — help yourself... How's your mother? I haven't seen her for some time, y'know. Last time was in London. England always takes me back to when I was small. A long time ago… but I do visit… of course it's a shame that you and I haven't had a chance to catch up recently. A grandfather should spend time with his grandson… But you've been there and I've been here, and we've both been here and there.

How're the women in your life? You have that lovely girlfriend — Susan? Shelley, OK. Ah right. Well, that's how it goes. You know something about literature of course. Jane Austen wrote at the start of *Pride and Prejudice* that "It is a truth universally acknowledged that a single man in possession of a good fortune must be in want of a wife." Well, I believe that certainly… but don't be in too much of a hurry. Have some fun… You are? Good.

What time is your flight? That's fine then… we have plenty of time. I wanted to have this time together. We could walk or stay here… It's very wet outside and humid, so perhaps let's stay here. You asked on the phone about some of the things that I'd been doing since we last met. Well, I thought about that a lot too — and, if you have the appetite, and the patience — I'd like to tell you about a few things that I've thought about. But not just since we last met. I was considering famous moments in history. Important moments. Someone asked me not that long ago if I'd ever found my job boring and she wondered if I would have preferred something more interesting. More challenging, she suggested. Challenging and interesting, sure. Boring, never.

I've been very fortunate to have been there at notable moments in time — and those moments are forever etched in my mind… remarkable moments in history, but from another point of view.

THE OTHER SIDE OF HISTORY

Mine. Seeing things from where I was. From where I happened to be. And defined by the people I was with at the time. Most definitely that. At every moment in time when something of importance has ever happened, there's always another story of what happened — behind the scenes. A lot of my experience has been behind the scenes or offstage. We don't always hear those stories. And in many ways that's a good thing because then one isn't on stage, as it were, in the direct line of fire. So sometimes — in fact, often — it's good to be away from the main action. You understand?

Yes, of course you can, dear boy. Please, help yourself — they're for you…

So that's what I want to talk to you about… if you will allow it… moments in history where important things happened, were happening or were about to happen, in or close to where I was at the time. Chance? Fortune? Luck? Happenstance? I guess so. All of those. Serendipity too. I believe in that. We seek things and sometimes things seek us. We're there, even if we don't ask to be. And sometimes we sure as merry hell don't want to be.

Where to start… where to even begin… Well, you know I started out in hotels when I was fifteen, nearly sixteen. My mother, your great-grandmother, was furious. I'd been well-educated, mostly in Britain, then in the States. But one day I just took off. There was no poverty-stricken upbringing, although my folks weren't at all wealthy. There was no abuse, no deep-rooted problem, no pain. I loved my parents and they me. I just wanted to go see things. I've just got the urge to go. To go off and explore! Not the smartest move, not initially anyway. And my poor folks — they were worried sick, of course. But they did forgive me eventually — and I did OK. And they knew that.

Let me tell you first a little about hotels. I've been in them all my working life — as you know of course. Everyone, or nearly everyone, in the world has stayed in at least one hotel or some accommodation away from home. People *like* staying in hotels, no matter what they say — even the jaded philanderers or spoilt professionals who are used to five-star hotels and business class air travel. I don't really know why — even after all these years. Maybe it's the anonymity, the "do what you want" feeling, the regular hot water (usually), the little bottles of shampoo, the miniature drinks, the convenience, the crisp sheets, sometimes the pillows, the sex, the love (they don't always go together of course), the wanting to be somewhere else or someone else... and people behave differently in hotels than they do at home. The fact that many often choose to behave badly is what makes them so interesting — the hotels, that is, not necessarily the people.

Well, now. Let's see. You have enough to drink? OK, good. So, Salvador Dalí was completely nuts when he stayed at Hotel Le Meurice in Paris, apparently bringing in animals and half-naked women, and then drawing on the walls. Got your attention now? I'm not certain if all that's true, but you get the picture or certainly *a* picture. Well, you can bet he wasn't doing all that in his own house. Which highlights another reason why people often have no respect for hotel rooms: someone else will clean it all up and there is a distinct pleasure in finding your hotel room all spick and span when you return in the evening after a busy day working or being a tourist.

Of course, it isn't the fault of the hotels that unusual events sometimes take place within their walls. In fact, it's usually a compliment. The better the hotel, the more shocking and juicy the scandal. Top hotels attract the rich and famous, and they drink too much, they take many substances up their noses — and generally behave badly. Sometimes more than badly. These occurrences, if they become public, usually raise a hotel's profile, often making it legendary. I know that applies to many American hotels, particularly those in New York... my home town. And yours, of course.

Some hotels embrace these events as part of their folklore. The Beverly Hills Hotel on Sunset Boulevard with its pink stucco is home to dozens of odd Hollywood tales. This hotel seems rather proud that Mariah Carey allegedly went through her breakdown there. Or that the billionaire Howard Hughes rented bungalows over long periods of time. He paid as much as $350,000 a year (more than two million dollars in today's money) to rent three bungalows: one for his wife, one for his bodyguards and one for himself. Hughes was highly reclusive and rumour has it that when he ordered his roast beef sandwiches, he would ask them to be left in the fork of a tree in the garden so he could fetch them unseen.

Then there's The Biltmore Hotel in Coral Gables, Miami, that opened in 1926 as a fashionable establishment attracting the likes of the Duke and Duchess of Windsor and Cornelius Vanderbilt. During the Second World War, it was converted into an army hospital — and ghosts of dead soldiers supposedly still haunt the building. Who knows? But one ghost is more enduring than others — that of Al Capone. The gangster stayed there at the height of his notoriety and the top floor Everglades Suite is known as the Al Capone Suite. In true mobster style, the suite has rotating walls that reveal gambling tables and a secret stairway for quick getaways. These walls have been sealed off though, so guests have to take the hotel's word for it that they do exist. I suppose I could tell you whether they do or don't, but I'm not going to… Sure, you can laugh. The ominous sounding 13th floor was once a speakeasy. One Capone crony, Fats Walsh I think it was, met his sticky end there. Some guests swear the elevator will occasionally stop on the 13th floor without the button being pushed. Stories like that are good for business.

The Carlyle Hotel in New York City has had its fair share of drama too. Princess Diana stayed at the hotel whenever she was in town. Woody Allen used to play clarinet for the jazz band in the café there nearly every Monday. John F. Kennedy Jr. ate breakfast there just before his last fateful flight — and actually the Carlyle is best known as the haunt of the elder Kennedys. Family patriarch Joe Kennedy maintained a suite at the hotel and his son, JFK, stayed at The Carlyle so often that it was dubbed the New York White House. His suite was never rented unless the hotel checked with him or his people first. The Carlyle is where Kennedy wound up after his legendary 45th birthday party at Madison Square Garden. To this day, there are persistent rumours about a series of hotel tunnels, which some say were used to usher women in and out of the hotel for both Kennedy *père et fils* (especially, it's claimed, Marilyn Monroe).

Its equal in Washington D.C. would be the Watergate Complex, which contains a hotel, apartments and offices. It is one of the city's most exclusive addresses, yet its very name is synonymous with the word "scandal". During the 1972 presidential campaign, its office compound was the site of the Democratic National Committee's headquarters, and it was bugged to monitor the opposition's campaign strategies. A burglary at the DNC office resulted in an FBI investigation which uncovered the bugging devices and that these illegal activites were carried out with President Richard Nixon's complicity. Nixon resigned in disgrace two years later. They made a movie about it — you seen it? Well, more than 20 years after that, the Watergate was again attached to scandal when it was revealed that Monica Lewinsky was living there. You know about her, right?

The St. Francis Hotel in San Francisco — now that has seen its fair share of scandalous events too. On Labour Day in 1921, silent film star Roscoe "Fatty" Arbuckle and his friend Fred Fishbach were partying in Suites 1219-1221. You won't know of Arbuckle I guess, but he was a big star back in the twenties. A young starlet named Virginia Rappe also attended the party — she died of internal injuries four days later. Arbuckle was accused of injuring her during a sexual assault, although he was tried three times and never convicted (two hung juries and an acquittal). The trial ended his career though, due in large part to William Randolph Hearst's inflammatory coverage of the trials. Newspapers hug scandals, don't they?

In 1950, the 64-year-old entertainer Al Jolson died in the same hotel shortly after a card game in a penthouse suite. In 1975, The St. Francis was also the location where deranged would-be assassin Sarah Jane Moore fired a shot at then President Gerald Ford. I reckon that nowadays very few guests mention Arbuckle or Ford. They will have more people asking if the hotel still washes coins or if J. Lo is staying there… Yes, here's an interesting thing… during the thirties and forties, the hotel employed people to literally wash coins so that ladies' white gloves wouldn't get dirty! For the record, the hotel might still do this upon special request. Now that's one way to launder money. OK, OK… I know.

Few hotel names carry the weight of the Waldorf Astoria in New York. We've been there several times — remember? Course you do. Established in 1893 by William Astor, this hotel became the world's largest and tallest hotel back in the thirties. By 1955, Hollywood's darling, Marilyn Monroe, had moved in full-time there with her then husband, Arthur Miller. In addition to its star-studded clientele, the hotel is also known for its food. Legend has it the hotel is the birthplace of the Waldorf Salad and 24-hour room service. You do? You want one now? No... personally I'm not that keen.

Where next? Well, walking down the grand staircase and into The Carlton Hotel New York's lobby is like taking a leap back in time. Back in 1904, the Beaux Arts building, then known as The Hotel Seville, is — or certainly was — one of the most opulent hotels in the States. Guests can pull up a stool at the same bar where Frank Sinatra used to listen to live music. Then there's the New York Hilton Midtown. In 1964, the penthouse suite was the home base for The Beatles whilst they were in town. Years later, John Lennon wrote *Imagine* there on hotel stationery. The press conference following the first cellphone call was held at the hotel in 1973 — and in 1998 the property introduced swipe cards that would eventually replace traditional room keys. They were one of the first hotels to do that. Clever. Although in those early days they didn't always work.

The Plaza in South Central Park is the setting for several chapters in *The Great Gatsby* and most notably it features in the movie, *Home Alone 2*. Sometimes celebrities check into hotels and stay put. New York's Hotel Elysée played home from home host to Marlon Brando, Maria Callas, Joe DiMaggio and Tennessee Williams. Many of Jack Kerouac's famous travel novels weren't written on the road. *The Subterraneans* and *Tristessa* were written while Kerouac was staying at The Marlton in Greenwich Village.

Lots of actors stayed there like Mickey Rourke and Maggie Smith. Lenny Bruce more or less lived there.

Hotels have been the settings of many memorable movies, from Alfred Hitchcock's *To Catch A Thief*, to Sofia Coppola's Tokyo tale *Lost in Translation* and onwards to Wes Anderson's fictional and so, so wonderful *Grand Budapest Hotel*. You haven't? Well you absolutely must. It's a superb movie and, if you like gothic tales set in middle Europe, this is perfect. Beautifully shot and cleverly framed. You've seen Hitchcock's *Psycho* and The Bates Motel? And there's the Overlook Hotel in Stanley Kubrick's *The Shining*.

San Diego's Brooklyn Hotel was built in the mid-1880s to accommodate a growing number of visitors and travellers — following the lengthening line of the transcontinental railroad. Wyatt Earp, the notorious lawman of the American West, arrived in San Diego in, what was it, 1886 I think. Yes, you're right — always been good with dates. Always kept diaries too. You know that. All of this stuff's in my diaries... Well now, Earp and his wife, Josephine, lived at The Brooklyn Hotel for nearly seven years. He may have been a famous gunman, but he spent a lot of time speculating in the local real-estate boom — opened gambling halls and saloons and the like. Read up on him. An interesting character and an interesting life.

The American writer Ernest Hemingway made

his first visit to Cuba in the twenties and lived there on and off throughout the thirties, staying at the Hotel Ambos Mundos. He particularly enjoyed Room 511's balcony view of Old Havana and in this room he began to write *For Whom the Bell Tolls*. The room is a shrine to Hemingway and you can still see his Remington typewriter and his bill from the hotel's bar — not that small I might add. One day please visit Cuba. It's a remarkable country and the music is fabulous. I remember your grandmother and I stayed in Santiago in Cuba, oh way back — some great times: the annual carnival brings fabulous costumes, excitement and great music to the town. Another place I loved in Cuba was Baracoa. A 500-year old bayside, riverside, beachside, mountainside village — it's been inhabited by indigenous Taino people who've been there for thousands of years. It genuinely is like a paradise. Ecologically perfect, absolutely beautiful and unique like nothing else in the world. The people are warm, simple, humble and hospitable... well now, that was quite a long time ago.

Agatha Christie wrote several mysteries set in hotels, including *Evil Under the Sun* and *At Bertram's Hotel*. One of her own favourite hotels was Istanbul's Pera Palace. Her then husband, Max Mallowan, was an archaeologist and the couple stayed at the Pera during his travels to excavations in the Middle East. Christie sat in room 411 and wrote *Murder on the Orient Express*.

Then there's Raffles Hotel in Singapore and that's famous for its colonial style, its museum and Victorian-style theatre. It's also a fantastic landmark. Sir Stamford Raffles was modern Singapore's

founder back in 1819. The hotel's famous for the Singapore Sling…
Oh you have? Want one now? Sure? The bartender who created this
nectar was a guy called Ngiam Tong Boon. What? Oh I guess around
1910 or thereabouts. It was also the setting for Ryū Murakami's
novel and film *Raffles Hotel*, which was filmed on location.

Most cities of the world and some towns have wonderful hotels,
not because of their fame, but because they're just good quality
hotels. And so many hotels hide secrets because they had a small
part to play in history, not always facing the lights but offstage or,
sometimes of course, part of the stage. I guess that most hotels
allow anyone to be anonymous — more or less — and maybe
that's why the hidden parts of historical moments can be found
in or near hotels. Plus of course the convenience — bedrooms,
meeting rooms, conference rooms, restaurants, coffee shops, places
to meet, quiet places to plan, to plot and to placate… to conspire
too. To hide. To love… To lose oneself.

But the key thing is that all hotels are points in and of history.
History of some kind. Well, history of all kinds of course. But I'm
referring to history that we all consider very important in one way
or another. Key historical moments. The hotels act as a backdrop
— a stage set. It's theatre. Sure, the scene changes — as do the
"performances", the actors, the extras, the props and the scripts
that are sometimes misplaced…

More sandwiches? Cake? OK then. Let me give you a sample
of my experiences observing history from the backstage, or
watching from the sides…

THE OTHER SIDE OF HISTORY

Buenos Aires,
August 1951

DON'T CRY
FOR ME ARGENTINA:

EVA PERÓN'S LAST
BROADCAST

It was in 1951 and one of my first jobs was in Buenos Aires. I spoke English mostly, of course, but I had a talent for languages and could switch easily. Guests like that. I was never condescending or rude. The hotel manager in New York — who liked me and my abilities to make customers feel at home — gave me the chance to go to South America where his brother worked at a sister hotel in Argentina's capital city. I hadn't travelled much — only Britain and the U.S., so this was a big journey. And don't forget Buenos Aires was the Paris of the 1950s. Well, Paris was the Paris of the 1950s, but the rich and famous liked Buenos Aires for the shops, the culture and the hotels. There may have been other reasons of course, perhaps relating to the end of the world war. You understand?

In August 1951, I was working as a bellhop — and I have to tell you my uniform was wonderful! A red cap set at a jaunty angle and red trousers with a blue tunic top and yellow scarf! Here look on the wall. There. No, that one. You've seen it before. That's me — standing next to the woman with her arm round my shoulder. See? Smart huh? Well... the noise in the streets in those days. The vibrant air. The cars. The people. The smells — the flowers, the perfumes and a hundred different aftershaves. The money.

In March of that year in the United States, there was the trial of Julius and Ethel Rosenberg for conspiracy to commit espionage. That same year saw United Artists releasing a sci-fi film called *The Man from Planet X*. Terrible. Armistice negotiations in Kaesong set off the beginning of the end of Korean War. King Abdullah I of Jordan was assassinated. Iran and Britain signed a big oil deal. Ted Kennedy was apparently caught cheating in an exam and had to leave Harvard. Yes, JFK's older brother. Winston Churchill was elected Prime Minister of the United Kingdom for a second term. India considered Kashmir as its territory, but held only half of it. Pakistan and China held the other parts. Pakistan claimed the part that India held, Jammu-Kashmir, because the majority of the people there were Muslim. *The Catcher in the Rye* was published. You haven't? Well, you damn well should. All these things had consequences, but then everything does of course. Everything does.

The hotel in which I worked was large and first class. It was expensive even then and the clientele had money. Loads of it. All cash. No credit cards in those days. Movies were shown in-house

— in a theatre downstairs, but most people listened to the radio.

It was a hot day even that early in the morning. A man came into the hotel lobby and beckoned me over. That wasn't unusual. It was my job to be beckoned over, to run errands, to give messages. My Spanish was fluent you know. Less good now, alas. The man said, "My name is General José Domingo Molina Gómez. In a moment an important lady will come in and there will be much fuss unless we are very careful."

The general (although I had to take his word for it because he was dressed in a sharp brown suit, crisp white shirt and blue tie, no uniform) lowered his sunglasses. "She may be disguised," he said quietly, "and you will take her to room 301. 301. Everything is arranged. You will not talk to her. There will be two men nearby. They are her guards. If anyone stops you, they will deal with the problem, but you must keep going, from here to the elevator to the third floor and then to the room. Here is the key."

The man held the key up in the air as if it were the Holy Grail. "Once at the room," he growled leaning in towards me, "you will open the door and let the woman in. Then give her the key and leave. Just leave. Here." He put the key in my left hand and clasped my fingers around it. He peered even closer at me. "I am told," he said slowly, "I am told that you are a smart young man. American yes?" I nodded. "You will talk to nobody about this mission. This I ask of you. Nobody. Do you understand?" I nodded and said that I did understand. He gave me a long look, still holding my hand clasping the room key.

The man made to move off, but suddenly turned, walked back to me and said, "You don't speak to this woman. You speak to *nobody* about this." And then he smiled and drew his hand across his throat. It's the kind of thing people do in bad movies. But he really did it and it frightened me as it was designed to do. I'd like to say that he had a gold tooth and a scar down his cheek, but he didn't. Then he left.

I stared after the man for a while, then looked round to see who was in the vicinity. There was no one. It was still early in the morning and there were perhaps a few guests strolling towards breakfast. Just people walking about, nobody taking notice of anything. I went about my business — and thought about the man, the woman, the room and the key — which I was still clutching in my hand.

As I was saying, Argentina was a wealthy place, for the rich certainly. There were violent gangs — the *barra bravas* they were called, but they were more into football villainy. There were other underworld gangs, mafia-like, some trading in drugs, others focusing on blackmail and prostitution. I didn't know if I was being set up for some reason — or maybe I was part of something that would cause my imminent arrest — or worse! Should I report the matter to my boss, a kindly man who had been very good to me? I made up my mind and was just about to leave the lobby to go my manager's office when two men came into the hotel and between them was a beautiful woman wearing a light blue skirt, with a matching jacket, white blouse, white shoes and sunglasses.

The three people moved quickly and straight for me. I stood still, terrified and one of the men indicated that I should lead the way — and fast! I quickly went to the elevators and we got in. There was one of our elevator guys, as smartly dressed as I — and he knew me of course. He looked from one person to another and thankfully had enough sense not to say or ask anything. I told him which floor we needed and he pulled the gates closed and pressed the button. Nobody spoke. I tried to smile at the lady, but she was wearing sunglasses and anyway just looked at the floor. The men were wearing sunglasses too — even more like a bad spy movie. They stood facing me. One of them had cut himself shaving and had a bit of tissue paper stuck just above his lip.

Well, we arrived at the third floor and I led them to the allocated room, unlocked the door and let one of the men in; the other one and the woman were left with me. The man came out, nodded to the other guy and the woman who then walked in. I handed the key to one man as the woman whispered something to the other. He nodded and turned to me and spoke to me in Spanish. He didn't smile, took off his sunglasses and looked straight into my eyes. "This lady will be collected in one hour by two other men. My friend here will stay outside the door to the room until then. She wants you to stay for a few moments in case she needs anything from the hotel. If she wants coffee, you get it. A sandwich, that's you. But you don't speak unless she speaks to you. You understand this? OK?"

I nodded. Then the man smiled and I could see that he had a

gold tooth (no really!), like a gangster or a character out of James Bond's world. He gave me a hundred dollar note. American. I shook my head, but his smile slipped and he stepped forward. I took the money. It was a lot of money for me. I turned to the room and the door was now shut. The guard sat on a chair and ignored me. Gold Tooth walked off, lighting a cigarette as he went. I paced the floor and hoped fervently that one of the managers wouldn't see me. I was also worried that I would be missed in the lobby. The hotel was run as a tight ship. Suddenly my own manager came round the corner and he was walking along the corridor right towards me. I froze. He got closer and, as he passed, he smiled and patted my shoulder. Then he walked on, nodding towards the guard who nodded back! Nothing happened. I had no clue what was going on or who the lady was, but I was certainly reassured that my manager was seemingly OK with everything. Unless he'd lost his marbles.

The room door suddenly opened and the lady looked out. She wasn't wearing her sunglasses now. She beckoned me over and I dutifully went. She smiled at me and her smile was contagious. She ushered me into the room. I looked at the guard but he didn't seem bothered. The room was tidy. She'd been sitting at the desk and there were papers with handwriting all over the desk and some on the floor.

"You are American?" she asked in Spanish. I nodded. "I don't like Americans as a rule," she said, "but I want to know what an outsider thinks. Follow the people… What's your name?" I told her.

"*Quiero que leas algo por favor.* I want you to read something,

THE OTHER SIDE OF HISTORY

please," she said, "And tell me, as an impartial American, what you think." She looked hard at me. "But the truth. I only want the truth." She stared a little more at me and then handed me a sheet of paper. "Sit down, please," she said. "Take off your hat." I sat, took off my hat and read:

"My beloved *descamisados* (a term of pride, originally meaning 'the shirtless ones'): Today is a day of many emotions for me. With all my soul I wanted to be with you and Perón on this glorious day… I have only one valuable thing and I have it in my heart. It burns my soul, it hurts my body and smarts my nerves. This is the love for this people. If the people asked me for my life, I would be happy to give it — because a life of one *descamisado* is worth more than my entire life.

"I have made, my friends, the irrevocable decision to renounce the honour which the workers and the people have bestowed upon me. I cannot accept. I must reject it. My frailty will not allow it. I cannot allow it. My husband, Perón, is the one who must lead you. That my people may say, when this wonderful chapter of history is written and surely dedicated to Perón, that at the side of Perón, there was a woman who was dedicated to bringing to the President, the hopes of the people. There is a woman alongside General Perón who took to him the hopes and needs of the people to satisfy them, and her name is Evita. But she cannot… I cannot serve you…"

I looked up. I knew a little about Eva Perón. I started to say something, blushing bright red.

"It's very… strong, powerful, señora. But I am no expert. I am not a politician and I am not… not one of your people. But it is… very, very strong. Is it a speech?" I felt very stupid not being able to offer much more than that. But hey, I was very young and in those days not a little awkward.

"It is a radio broadcast," said Eva Perón. "My notes… I must finish it now… ¿*Entiendes la emoción?* Do you understand the emotion in it?"

"Yes, señora, I do… I… do." Just then there was a firm knock on the door and the guard came in and spoke in fast Spanish. Eva Perón nodded and took my hand, shook it and thanked me, indicating that I should go, which of course I did. And that was that.

I went downstairs and saw my manager. He walked me to the edge of the lobby and said, "You know, she starts her morning very early in her office at the Secretaria de Trabajo y Previsión and the first part of her day lasts until four in the afternoon. At five she's back and continues to work until dawn with only a few short breaks. She is loved by the people… and… she is very ill." Just then two new men rushed in and spoke to my manager who nodded and went off with the men towards the elevator.

Well, I heard the radio broadcast that Eva Duarte de Perón made on August 31, 1951 — the radio address known as the *Renunciamiento*. With a faltering, almost broken voice, she declined irrevocably the honour of the vice presidency and hinted that her time as the country's chief Peronista was near its end. It was unquestionable that you could truly feel Evita's presence through her voice. She declared her one true ambition — hang on a

THE OTHER SIDE OF HISTORY

moment, I've got my diary here — let me read this: "That my people may say, when this wonderful chapter of history is written and surely dedicated to Perón, that at the side of Perón, there was a woman who was dedicated to bringing to the President, the hopes of the people." She had I guess that special gift that some great people have of making you feel as if they are talking only to you and you alone.

In 1952, shortly before her death from cancer at the very young age of 33, Eva Perón was given the title of Spiritual Leader of the Nation by the Argentine Congress. She had a state funeral, something generally reserved for heads of state. I was there. I wasn't sure what to feel. I didn't necessarily side with her politics — or actually anyone's politics in those days — but I had seen and read a little of her passion and what she really felt in her heart. Immediately after her death, the government suspended all official activities for two days and ordered all flags flown at half-mast for ten days. It seemed, however, that these things fell short of reflecting popular grief. The crowd outside the presidential residence, where Evita died, grew dense, congesting the streets for ten blocks in all directions. They say something like three million people attended her funeral. The streets of Buenos Aires overflowed with huge piles of flowers. Within a day of her death, all florists in Buenos Aires had run out of flowers.

SNAKE HIPS:

ELVIS PRESLEY CUTS HIS FIRST RECORD

Look, these sandwiches are for you. Let's get more tea. Or something else? It's still raining… No, we have plenty of time.

Anyway, that was Eva Perón. Let's see… where next? Memphis, 1953 and I was working at the Peabody Hotel in Union Avenue… yessir — seeing the world and loving it! Peabody history dates back to 1869, when the original Peabody Hotel opened on the corner of Main and Monroe, and immediately became the social and business hub of Memphis. Well, in 1925 a newer, grander Peabody was built at Union and 2nd Street — continuing the legacy of the South's Grand Hotel. Here's a thing. It was in 1933 when ducks were originally put in the hotel's lobby fountain, setting up a tradition that continued with the March of the Peabody Ducks. Still there.

I liked Memphis. Still do. There were a few recording studios near the hotel and also close to where I lived then — in a boarding house run by a wonderfully full-of-life widow called Agnes Daley. She had bleached hair and was as wide as she was tall. Embarrassed as I am now to say it, she tried to seduce me on more than one occasion. Ha. Don't look at me like that. As it was, nothing happened…

It was July and the afternoon was warm and humid. Few people about. I was walking home. Sun Studio was also in Union Avenue… 706 Union Avenue… It's a recording studio and you could usually hear some guitar and country and western stuff floating down the street from one or other of the studios — Carl Perkins was popular, as was Johnny Cash. Sun Records was a small record label mostly promoting Memphis blues and country songs. They also ran a recording service for artists or anyone who came off the streets to record a song for a fee of $3.98 which, even in those days, wasn't a lot. My friend at the hotel used to dare me to go in and record something, but he knew as well as do you that I can't much hold a note let alone a whole song. No, nice of you to say, but we both know that it simply ain't so!

Well, so… you could walk in and make a two-sided record. I have to say that I was often tempted, but never did it. Anyways, as I walked by there on that late afternoon, I saw a guy looking through the Sun Records window. As I passed, he turned and smiled. I smiled back. Then he said, "Sir, ma apologies, but do you know what tahm these people open up in the mornin'?"

I said that I didn't, but guessed that it wouldn't be too early and told him. He looked a little crestfallen.

I asked, "Forgive me for asking, but are you going to record something?"

"Nah," he said and looked at the floor chewing his lip. "Thought ah would but, ah dunno."

"Can you sing?" I asked.

"Well, folks say ah caint, but ah think sure ah cain."

"Well, maybe you should do it anyway. Only four dollars."

"Yeah, I know. Mebee. Hey, do *you* sing?"

I laughed and told him no. He didn't laugh back.

"Ah reckon all folks can sing if they wants to. Jest needs to believe a little."

"Do you go to school round here?"

"Just graduated from Humes High."

"Did you sing there?"

"Sure did… and at church on Sundays."

"Has anyone told you that you have a good voice?"

"Some." He jerked a thumb at Sun Records. "Hopin' to get a chance here."

"Well, I hope you do OK. Maybe I'll buy your records one day. What's your name?"

Well, Elvis chose *My Happiness* and *That's When Your Heartaches Begin* to sing for his first record. Amazingly, both tracks and his follow-up recording in July 1954 of *I'll Never Stand In Your Way / It Wouldn't Be The Same (Without You)* survived and are available

THE OTHER SIDE OF HISTORY

on CD to this day. I have them somewhere…

The next late afternoon, as usual I walked past Sun Records and, out of curiosity, went in asked the receptionist if a Mr. Presley had been in that day. She said that he had and asked if I was a friend of his. I said I wasn't really, but had met him the day before. Apparently she had asked what kind of singer he was to which Elvis had replied, "Ah sing all kinds." When she pressed him on what singer he sounded like, he answered, "Ah don't sound like nobody." After he had recorded, Sun boss Sam Phillips asked Marion, the receptionist, to note down the young man's name, which she did along with her own commentary: "Good ballad singer. Hold."

Well, not so long after that, Presley failed an audition for a local vocal quartet, the Songfellows. He explained to his father, "They told me ah couldn't sing." Songfellow member, Jim Hamill, later said that Elvis was turned down because he didn't demonstrate an ear for harmony. Extraordinary how these things work out. Elvis began working for the Crown Electric Company as a truck driver. After playing a few local gigs with him, his friend Ronnie Smith suggested that he contact Eddie Bond, leader of Smith's band, which had an opening for a vocalist. Bond allegedly rejected him after a tryout, advising Elvis to stick to truck driving "because you're never ain't gonna make it as a singer."

Then Sam Phillips received a song from Nashville music publisher Sam Wortham, the same person who had delivered *Just Walking In The Rain*, Sun Record's first big hit record by The Prisonaires. Phillips heard something in this new song, but he couldn't find the singer on the demo, so he finally decided that it just might fit the young man about whom Marion kept reminding him. The song was called *Without You*, an OK but unexceptional ballad. The date was June 26, 1954. Marion phoned Elvis asking if he could come down to the studio. Elvis later said that he ran all the way. I can imagine him doing just that! But, try as he did, he just couldn't get the song right. This could have been the final rejection, the ultimate disappointment, the last straw, if not for Sam's belief in raw talent and his desire to uncover it. Elvis did record one song for his mother's birthday called *My Happiness* but that was more or less it. Sam had this real feeling that the boy had something though and invited Elvis to sing everything he knew. Sam talked about it with Scotty Moore, guitarist in the group The Starlite Ranglers. Sam told Scotty to check Elvis out and gave him Elvis' phone number. The rest as they say is more or less history I guess.

You know... Sam Phillips was an interesting guy. He'd been thinking more and more that the key to a new sound in popular music lay in the connection between the races, you know black and white and in what they had in common far more than what kept them apart. There were always going to be unpleasant white people, he knew, but far more to the point was the spiritual connection that he had always known to exist between black people and white folks — the cultural heritage that they all shared. He had begun to talk increasingly to Marion about finding someone, and it had to be a white man, because the wall that he had run into with his recordings practically proved that in the racial climate then, someone black was unlikely able to bridge the gap.

One song continued to haunt Sam, a plaintive ballad called *Without You* that the song publisher Red Wortham had given him. There was something about it — for all of its sentimentality, there was a quality of vulnerability, and he thought that he'd like to have someone come in and give it a try. The only one who came to mind was a kid who had stopped by the previous summer and for $4 cut a "personal" record for his mom.

Well, the "kid" had come in to cut another "personal" around six months or so after the first. And after that he evidently stopped by from time to time to talk with Marion. Sam was well aware of that fact because Marion did keep talking about him. Sam didn't really know, but when Marion brought up his name for what seemed like the thousandth time, he thought, well, hell, why not? The boy had the same yearning quality in his voice, attached to the kind of fervour that you might be more inclined to assign to gospel music. Sam had no idea of the boy's full potential, but there was no question, he was different. So he had Marion call him.

Elvis Presley came into the studio. He was 19 years old, a good-looking boy — long sideburns, greased hair combed in a ducktail at the back that he kept patting down. But what struck Sam most was the genuine humility — humility mixed with determination. He was, Sam thought, one of the most introverted people who had ever come into the studio, but for that reason one of the bravest, too. He reminded Sam of many of the great early blues singers and that "his insecurity was so markedly like that of a black person."

Presley's first single was *That's All Right* — and it's the song that made his name overnight really. Not long afterwards, the record company RCA Victor acquired his contract in a deal arranged by Colonel Tom Parker who managed the singer for more than two decades. Presley's first RCA single, *Heartbreak Hotel* was released in January 1956 and became a number-one hit in the United States.

Memphis was a happy home to a diverse musical scene: gospel, blues, hillbilly, country, boogie and western swing. Not sure either you or I know fully what they are, but still. Taking advantage of this range of talent, there were no style limitations at the label. In one form or another Sun recorded them all. While I was in Memphis I did keep up with the people at Sun Records, not least because the music was mostly good, but also because I got on well with Marion Keisker who was great and obviously so proud of her "find". She passed away in December 1989.

Sun Records? Yeah, that's still going. The company is in business now running as Sun Entertainment Corporation. The music of many Sun Records musicians helped lay part of the foundation of late 20th century rock 'n' roll and influenced many younger musicians, including The Beatles. In 2001, Paul

McCartney appeared on a tribute album called *Good Rockin' Tonight: The Legacy of Sun Records*. Look over there — it's a copy of the famous photograph of Carl Perkins, Johnny Cash and Jerry Lee Lewis grouped round Elvis Presley at the piano, the night when the four joined in an impromptu jam at Sun Record's one-room sound studio, December 4, 1956. You should go to Memphis one time — for more than Elvis Presley.

STANDING UP
FOR HER RIGHTS:

ROSA PARKS DOES NOT
GIVE UP HER SEAT

Moving on. Moving on. More of Memphis in a while. In December 1955, I was working in Montgomery, Alabama. It was a quiet place and I had been promoted to meeting and greeting guests as they arrived. I would very often be used as an additional concierge guy and the regular concierge team insisted that I share my tips — which I did and, boy, they knew exactly how much was their due.

Next to the hotel was a bar run by a gent called Hugo Konkryke. Hugo was a mountain of a man, but was kindly and friendly. He also mixed a mean drink and he knew every kind of mixture from an Old Fashioned to a Mai Tai, and any beverage of dubious origin in-between. Mind you, I'm partial to a good dry Martini — has to be a slice of lime, mind, not lemon. Or maybe a Campari and soda — has to be a slice of orange in that, not lemon.

Well, the teams from the local bus company used to go to the bar for a drink at the end of their shifts. Sometimes I had to go there to fetch smokes for guests — the bar had all kinds of tobacco, more than what we sold at the hotel, and guests wanted precisely what they wanted.

Well, one afternoon, I went to the bar and it was very quiet. People used to talk to me there — y'know the kind of thing: "How's it going kid?", "Nice day, ain't it?", "Hiya son, s'up?" "Cool uniform, wanna swap?", "Got change for a five, kid?" They were all basically decent people and I liked their gentle humour and love for life. One in particular was always happy to let me sit at the bar, maybe have a quick soda on the house. His name was Kevin Able and he was a bus driver. He'd been with the bus company, the Montgomery City Lines, for years. Well, that afternoon, when I'd been sent for change, he told me a story about another bus driver, James Blake.

In those days, disgraceful as it was for any country — and absolutely no less for the United States — it was against the law in the U.S. for a black person to sit on a bus when a white person needed that seat. During one typical evening rush hour, a 42-year-old woman took a seat on the bus on her way home from the Montgomery Fair Department Store where she worked as a seamstress. Before she reached her destination, she quietly set off a social revolution when the driver, yes — James Blake, instructed her to move to the back of the bus so that standing white people could sit and she just refused. Just said no. Rosa Parks, an African American, was arrested that day for violating a city law requiring racial segregation of public buses.

I didn't know, but Kevin explained that on the city buses of Montgomery, the front ten seats were permanently reserved for white passengers. Mrs. Parks was seated in the first row behind those ten seats. When the bus became crowded, the bus driver, James Blake, instructed Mrs. Parks and the passengers seated in that row, all African Americans, to vacate their seats for the white passengers who were getting on the bus.

Eventually, three of the passengers moved, while Mrs. Parks remained seated, arguing that she was not in a seat reserved for whites. Mr. Blake believed he had the discretion to move the line separating black and white passengers. The law was actually somewhat obscure on that point, but when Mrs. Parks defied his order, he took action. He said that he had no choice. She was arrested. And she was charged with refusing to obey the orders of a bus driver.

Kevin said that there was history here. Twelve years prior to the 1955 incident, Parks boarded a bus again driven by Blake. She entered the front door of the bus and paid her fare. As she went on to take a seat, Blake told her to follow city rules and enter the bus again from the back door. After exiting the front door, she came around the back of the bus to use the rear entrance, only for Blake to drive off immediately. Parks sat and waited for the next bus to arrive. I wasn't sure then — or indeed now — that I cared much for Kevin's "friend", Blake. And I wonder, in truth, if Kevin felt that his colleague had done the right thing. Or the kind thing. But one doesn't know what any situation demands or whether James was doing the usual thing and "following orders". I have a distaste for the latter and the lack of humanity it involves, but this wasn't and isn't the worst example ever.

Anyway, on this day in December, Blake ordered Rosa Parks and three other black people to move from the middle to the back of his Cleveland Avenue bus in order to make room for one white male passenger. By Parks's account, Blake said, "Y'all better make it light on yourselves and let me have those seats." When she refused, Blake first contacted the bus company and then called his boss allegedly remarking, "I called the company first, just like I was supposed to do." And then he called the police. "I got my supervisor on the line. He said, 'Did you warn her, Jim?' I said, 'I warned her.' And he said, and I remember it just like I'm standing here, 'Well then, Jim, you do it, you got to exercise your powers and put her off, hear?' And that's just what I did."

Her arrest became a rallying point around which the local African American community organised a bus boycott to protest against the discrimination they had endured for years and years. Martin Luther King Jr., the 26-year-old minister of the Dexter Avenue Baptist Church, spoke out and emerged a leader during the peaceful boycott that lasted over a year.

After Mrs. Parks was convicted under city law, her lawyer filed a notice of appeal. While her case was tied up in the state court of appeals, a panel of three judges in the U.S. District Court for the region ruled in another case that racial segregation of public buses was unconstitutional. You're thinking no big deal, right? You're thinking, yeah that was pretty disgraceful for people not that long ago to have segregation. But you're also maybe thinking, "So what?" Well, I'll tell you so what. Rosa Parks's act of defiance and the famous Montgomery Bus Boycott became important symbols of the modern Civil Rights Movement. She became an international icon of resistance. An important moment in time.

I met Kevin only once again at the same bar. He was weary. He supported Rosa Parks and private citizens who were tired of giving in. He told me that she'd been fired from her job as a seamstress — and, God help us, had received death threats. But y'know, these things still happen today. Not necessarily in America but they happen all over the place and I'm guessing still do in America. Not on buses maybe, but elsewhere. To all kinds of folks. Anyway, the U.S. Supreme Court later declared that Alabama's bus segregation law was illegal.

It's over six decades since the civil rights icon took a historic stand on an Alabama bus. In 2005, after Rosa Parks had passed away aged 92, Barack Obama celebrated the woman's courage. Let me read something. He said, "Like so many giants of her age, Rosa Parks is no longer with us. But her lifetime of activism — and her singular moment of courage — continue to inspire us today. Refusing to give up a seat on a segregated bus was the simplest of gestures, but her grace, dignity, and refusal to tolerate injustice helped spark a Civil Rights Movement that spread across America…

Some schoolchildren are taught that Rosa Parks refused to give up her seat because her feet were tired. Our nation's schoolbooks are only getting it half right. She once said: 'The only tired I was, was tired of giving in.'... As a personal note, I think it is fair to say were it not for that quiet moment of courage by Mrs. Parks, I would not be standing here today. I owe her a great thanks, as does the Nation..." A good thing to say and I reckon he meant it.

What the hell happened to James Blake? Well, apparently he continued working at the bus company for another 19 years. He died in his Montgomery home in 2002, less than a month before his 90th birthday. Commenting on his death, Rosa Parks said, "I'm sure his family will miss him." A good thing to say and I reckon she meant it.

BETWEEN THE MEDITERRANEAN AND THE DEEP RED SEA:

NASSER SHUTS THE SUEZ CANAL

Well, let's see now. 1956. It was July 26. I was in Egypt. Alexandria. A new posting at the Cecil Alexandria Hotel in Saad Zaghloul Square, very close to the Manshia Square, the Attarine Mosque and St. Mark's Coptic Orthodox Cathedral. A lowly posting, but exciting nonetheless.

There was a crowd, tens of thousands, gathered in Manshia Square to hear a speech by Egypt's then president, Gamal Abdel Nasser. I wasn't sure whether to go because Egypt wasn't over-fond of Americans to say the least and my knowledge of Arabic was poor.

I was meant to meet up with two people who worked at the hotel and with whom I'd made friends. But we lost each other in the crowd. I had no real clue as to which way I should go and the crush was pretty bad. As I passed a side street, someone bumped into me from the front and another from the back. I apologised — normal reaction from me, I guess. The guy in front smirked and pushed me away. I discovered then that I was walletless! Of course the two thieves got clean away. I went hot, then cold, angry then frustrated and angry again — all in a matter of seconds. A policeman was looking at me, but seemed totally disinterested in helping me and I could have sworn that he'd seen the whole incident. The wallet didn't have a fortune in it, since I didn't get much in the name of money in those days, but I was trying to save what I had so the money's loss was still strongly felt. Plus it had some photographs of your great grandparents and my brothers and losing them was a big thing.

Someone tapped me on the shoulder. I looked up and saw a little man, reasonably well-dressed — beige suit, white shirt and green and red striped tie — and he was smiling at me, an open and friendly smile. He gestured that I should go down the side street with him. I wasn't keen to go anywhere strange with anyone strange, and really just wanted to get back to the safety of my hotel and feel sorry for myself. But the man was insistent and he had a small child with him — and I did very much want to get away from the crowd, so I followed.

In the quiet of the narrow, side street, the man said in a soft voice, "You English you?"

"No, sir," I said although I should have said yes in truth. Safer. "No," I said. "I'm American, but I work here."

"Where you work?" I wasn't sure if I could trust this little guy, but nonetheless I told him the name of the hotel still wondering if I was right to tell him anything at all when I should just get the hell away. The child looked up at me and smiled. "You want hear speech? You may be problems. Americans bad here," the man said pointing towards the square and the noise. Suddenly his little boy started crying and I thought it was because of the crowd and people bumping into him. The man picked up the boy.

"Is your boy frightened? The noise?"

The man nodded. "I have to be here. I must stay. Otherwise trouble... I have job... I must be here." He smiled. "I must be here," he said emphatically. "So he too. With me. Must be here. He have no mother." At this, he pointed at the little boy. I dug around in my jacket pocket and found a packet of root beer barrel candy which I was partial to in those days. My family had just sent a fresh supply over... You haven't? Well, I'll try and get some for you. Sure, you should! Well, anyway, I gave the packet to the little boy. Instantly, he stopped crying, wiped a grubby hand across an even grubbier nose and smiled a sunshine smile. He looked up at his father who nodded. The boy took the offered packet. The man smiled again at me and indicated that I should follow him.

"We go here. You listen Nasser?" He looked about him in a worried way. I nodded.

"Come. Come." He led me along a winding route of tiny passageways. There were few people here — only some elderly women and some children who regarded me with that direct, hard

THE OTHER SIDE OF HISTORY

stare that discomforts us all when we visit foreign lands. I was terrified that I would lose my guide because I now had absolutely no real clue where I was — and it was certainly way off the beaten track. I was sweating buckets by now and my bandana was soaked. After what seemed like a very long time, we arrived at a small square in what was obviously the back of the wide stage that had been erected for the big speech. Martial music was blaring out and the crowd was cheering at something that must have been going on, but what it was I couldn't see. There was a large group of soldiers here and I was obviously more than mildly nervous. A few of the soldiers looked at the man, the boy and then at me. One moved over and spoke to the man who talked quickly, peppering whatever he was saying with some finger-pointing in my direction. The little boy was happily eating the candy, clutching the packet tightly in his hand, his other in mine.

After what seemed like an endless conversation, the soldier nodded and went off back to his colleagues and had a quick chat with his commander. The little man turned to me. "Is OK," he said. "You stay. You keep still. You listen. Talk to no one. No one. I say you from Australia. Now I must go." I must have looked worried. "Is OK. OK." He shook his head. "No trouble for you. When finish, go straight back to... you hotel. Look..." and he pointed to a main road just ahead. "Turn right there and straight line. You find." He smiled again and shook my hand. The little boy grinned, showing me that he had a mouthful of candy, some of which was dribbling down his chin. He waved as the two made their way through the crowd.

I turned to look towards the soldiers and when I looked back, the man and his boy were gone. The soldier who'd talked to the man earlier came over. His English was good.

"You work at Cecil Alexandria Hotel?" I looked at him, astonished that he knew. I thought that I'd better agree so I did so in as much of a non-American accent as I could muster. Whether it sounded Australian or not I have no clue but it probably wouldn't have been a hit in Sydney.

The soldier smiled. "He is good man," he said, waving in the vague direction of the wider world. He went back to his group.

"Excuse me, sir," said a deep American voice behind me. I turned and there was a portly guy with a florid face and a huge spotted red bandana clutched against it. Straight out of central casting.

"I couldn't help overhearing your conversation, sir. James Gould, freelance reporter. At your service. Been here for nearly five years now. You're American too I take it?"

I nodded, but quickly asked him to speak more quietly.

He held out a large, fleshy hand. I shook it. "And you work at the Cecil, I hear. The guy who brought you here. You know who he is?"

"No sir, I don't." I wasn't sure a) whether I should or could trust this guy and b) if people could hear our accents.

The noise from the square suddenly went up a clutch of decibels and it was hard to hear the big man. He leaned in so that his fedora touched my forehead and I could smell the garlic, *arak* and cigarettes on his breath as he spoke. "The Cecil Hotel was built in 1929 by the French-Egyptian Jewish Metzger family as a romantic hotel for lovers, holidaying couples and the intelligentsia. All the great writers stayed there y'know — Somerset Maugham, Lawrence Durrell — plus folks like Winston Churchill and Al Capone, apparently. The British Secret Service kept a suite for their clandestine operations. Then the hotel was seized by the Egyptian government, after the revolution in 1952 and most of the Metzger family were expelled from the country. But one Metzger is left, although I suspect he too needs to leave soon. That was Albert Metzger. You just met him. His father built the hotel and Albert and his family are… were running it, but it's gradually being taken over by this guy…" At this juncture, James Gould jerked his thumb towards the stage and the square; any further conversation was simply impossible.

While I was interested in what the big guy had to say, I was pleased that he'd stopped talking because I was really terrified that someone would suddenly realise that we were Americans. The noise was huge now, an express train of a roar, but at the same time the atmosphere seemed tense. Mr. Gould tensed, the soldiers tensed too, clutching their rifles more tightly, and I certainly tensed. Tension was a natural state of affairs in Egypt's cities in those days. Only days before, Nasser had received a humiliating rebuff from the U.S. Secretary of State, John Foster Dulles, to his request for a loan to build the High Dam on the River Nile. Egypt had received a considerable quantity of weapons from the Czech Republic in 1955 and Dulles hoped to achieve two aims:

one, to humble Nasser, whose anti-colonial rhetoric was winning support across the Middle East; and two, to remind other aspiring Third World leaders that there was no neutral ground in what was becoming the Cold War.

Suddenly and seemingly from the front of house, there was a series of very loud barked military instructions and even more soldiers arrived, marching at a trot and leading Nasser to the stage via the back area where Gould and I were standing. The soldiers looked neither left nor right, but Nasser did, staring straight at me for a moment, flickering his gaze to take in Gould — and then he moved swiftly up some steps and towards the stage.

Now the noise was tremendous and truly deafening. Well, my journalist companion translated for me as Nasser hit his stride. The president joked with the crowd, describing Eugene Black, head of the World Bank, as a peddler of "mortgage colonialism". Black reminded him, he said, of Ferdinand de Lesseps, whose company had constructed the Suez Canal in the 19th century. As the crowd laughed, jeered and cheered, we later found out that Egyptian troops were at that very moment taking control of the Suez Canal Company's headquarters in Port Said. Apparently, repeated mention of Lesseps was a code for the military takeover of the Canal, but hell, I don't know. I think Nasser liked the sibilance of the name. He finished his speech with a simple statement — wait, I have it here: "Everything which was stolen from us by that imperialist company, that state within a state, when we were dying of hunger, we are going to take back... The government has decided on the following law: a presidential decree nationalizing the International Suez Canal Company. In the name of the nation, the president of the republic declares the International Suez Canal Company an Egyptian limited company."

Well, the crowd in Alexandria that day went super crazy and erupted with delight. Here at last was proof that the era of colonial domination was over: the greatest powers on earth would no longer determine Egypt's fate. I learned later that in Washington, Nasser's reply to Dulles was received with consternation. Dulles told Anthony Eden, the then British prime minister, that Nasser must "disgorge" the canal. Sure — funny turn of phrase. Dulles's reaction pales compared to the blind rage that echoed up from the leaders of the old imperialist powers, Britain and France. In London and Paris, politicians competed in insulting Nasser. Hugh Gaitskell, leader of the Labour Party, then in opposition in Britain, likened Nasser to Hitler. Anthony Eden made the same analogy, warning that, "We all know this is how fascist governments behave and we all remember only too well what the cost can be of giving in to fascism."

The Suez Crisis, as the events of the following months came to be called, marked the humiliating end of imperial influence for Britain and France. It cost the British Prime Minister, Anthony Eden, his job and, by showing up the shortcomings of the Fourth Republic in France, hastened the arrival of the Fifth Republic under Charles de Gaulle. It also strengthened the resolve of many Europeans to create what became the European Union. And it promoted pan-Arab nationalism on a huge scale and completed the transformation of the Israeli-Palestinian dispute into an Arab-Israeli one. It provided a distraction that encouraged the Soviet Union to put down an uprising in Hungary in the same year. *Plus ça change...*

If all this is difficult to understand... well, remember that the world was a different place then, in the mid-50s. Many European politicians still believed that their countries had an absolute right to run the affairs of others. Many were also scarred by memories of appeasement in the 1930s. Faced with a provocation — even an entirely legal one involving the nationalization of a foreign-owned asset like the Suez Canal — the instinct of such Europeans was to go to war. No question. They and their Israeli partners believed that an invasion was the only way to go, but they were eventually restrained by the firm hand that was the United States, led by a Republican president and war hero, Dwight Eisenhower.

In Egypt, the British had become so resented for their racist, arrogant ways that, by the early 1950s, even Winston Churchill, on his second term as prime minister, felt he could resist the tide of nationalism no more and wanted out. After 1951, the British were confined to the Suez Canal Zone, harassed by the Egyptians who wanted them out altogether. The last British soldiers left the zone in June 1956. The Israelis provided a solution, well — a solution of sorts. In September of 1956, a delegation secretly presented the French with a fabricated deal: that Israel would invade Egypt and race to the Suez Canal. The French and British could then invade the area with some legitimacy, posing as peacekeepers — to separate the two sides and occupy the Canal, ostensibly to guarantee the free passage of shipping. When this plan was presented to Anthony Eden, he jumped at it. It was a lifeline. The British and French forces now had a pretext to invade. For the Israelis, this would punish Egypt for its escalating incursions into Israel from Gaza. It would also ensure that the major European powers supported Israel. You have to remember that the French had always tried to be even-handed between Israel and its neighbours — and the British had leaned towards the Arab states.

So, in late October 1956, Israeli paratroopers were dropped into Sinai to fulfill their side of the bargain. Pretending shock and surprise, the British and French issued an ultimatum to both sides for an immediate ceasefire. When the Egyptians rejected this out of hand, British planes started bombing the Egyptian air force on the ground and, in November, Anglo-French troops went ashore to begin the invasion of the Suez Canal Zone and it was hoped that the result would be to topple Nasser. However, almost immediately, Eden surrendered to American angry demands and stopped the operation, with his troops stranded half way down the Canal. The French were furious, but had to agree; their troops were under British command. What had been a seemingly solid plan was turning into a total mess.

The United Nations assembled an international emergency force to go to the Suez Canal and monitor the ceasefire. These were to be the first UN peacekeepers. The organization was one of the clear winners of the crisis, gaining an enhanced role in the world. Britain, then Europe's strongest power, would, it seemed, always put its special relationship with America above its European interests. And the Americans, as far as the French were concerned, were both unreliable and annoyingly superior.

The British were beaten up most of all by the Suez Crisis. The episode ended Britain's remaining imperial pretensions once and for all, really — and hastened the independence of its colonies. Some talked of a Suez syndrome, where, in Margaret Thatcher's words many years later, Britain's rulers "went from believing that Britain could do anything to an almost neurotic belief that Britain could do nothing." The major lesson of Suez for the British was that the country would never be able to act independently of America again. True. Soon afterwards, the Russians duly stepped in to finance the Aswan Dam and much else in Egypt — and Israel became ever more closely tied to the United States.

The chief victor of Suez, in the short term certainly, was Nasser himself. Before the crisis, he'd faced lingering opposition in Egypt, not only from the former ruling class but also from communists and the radical Islamists of the Muslim Brotherhood. "Pulling the Lion's tail" and, more to the point I guess, getting away with it, was very popular in Egypt. The country projected itself as the vanguard of Arab nationalism and a beacon to liberation movements across the Third World. Saddam Hussein was one who drew huge inspiration from this. Of course, as I'm sure you know, Nasser himself was eventually largely discredited by Israel's crushing victory of Egypt in the 1967 war.

Well now, history lesson over, but not uninteresting you'll agree. Ah yes, good question — what of Albert Metzger and indeed James Gould? Well, they worked in this business. Good people. Both now long gone, alas. Y'know, I met Albert's son a few years ago. He didn't recall the candy, but his smile was exactly the same… I have a picture here somewhere…

FOOD, GLORIOUS FOOD:

THE INSTANT NOODLE

This may not be a big deal to you, but it sure *is* a big deal to many. Dreamt up by Taiwan-born Momofuku Ando in Japan in 1958, the instant noodle created a cheap and speedy new food culture. By 2013, 105 billion packets were sold annually worldwide. 105 billion. That's a lot of noodles.

Yes, I was in Tokyo for a short while in the late fifties. You know, I'm sure, that Japan was still struggling with a shortage of food after the war. America supplied flour for bread, but bread wasn't a staple for the Japanese. Ando was sure that, if people had enough to eat, then the reconstruction of a ruined country could move apace. Made sense. I was working at a prime site Tokyo hotel and I met Ando there. My hotel was next to the Palace Hotel.

A historic, luxury hotel overlooking the Imperial Palace moat in the heart of Tokyo, with rooms that looked out over the palace gardens. It may be in the heart of the city — the economic and retail hub of Marunouchi — but its setting with its surrounding green grounds, creates a spacious, uncrowded feel.

What was I doing with noodles? Well, Ando was meeting some businessmen and he wanted to make a demonstration. He had asked for a regular supply of boiling water and some small bowls. I was directed to work with his assistant in the meeting room. I had no clue what was being demonstrated. I was told that it was a new food that had been flash-fried and dried which, when mixed with boiling water, would expand and become regular, delicious noodles. Sounded horrible.

Momofuku Ando was born Wu Baifu in Taiwan in 1910 and, after the Second World War, he emigrated to Japan and took on a new name. There, he undertook a variety of jobs — including selling socks and making salt — while in his spare time trying out all kinds of recipes that would help the food shortage problem. But it wasn't until he was in his forties that the ramen inspiration struck. Ramen, as I'm sure you know very well, is, in Japanese cuisine, quick-cooking noodles, typically served in a broth with meat and vegetables. Done well — delicious.

So OK. The businessmen all assembled and there was much bowing and smiling, apart from one shorter man who didn't smile at all. There were around 16 people in the room plus Ando, his assistant and me. I was dressed in kitchen whites, as was Ando and his assistant — the impression being, I guess, that we looked like chefs. I was in charge of the boiling water, which was in a large pot over something like a Bunsen burner.

Ando began to talk about his invention and that went on for some time. I had no clue as to what was being said. I was quite young and I suppose my attention span was a bit limited, especially when my Japanese was weak, but I tried very hard to look focused — and still. Ando had demanded that I stayed still. Then the patter finished and I was instructed to ladle boiling water into the 16 bowls of dried noodles. Ando stirred the noodles and the water. Not much happened. The 16 business guys looked impassive. Nobody was smiling now. I was told to hand out the bowls, which I duly did, helped by Ando's assistant. Nobody spoke. People picked up their chopsticks and bowls, gingerly putting noodles, now softened, in their mouths. Still nobody spoke. The man who hadn't smiled at the start looked around at his colleagues. Then one nodded and another and another. And then he smiled and tried some and smiled some more. Ando smiled. I think I did too.

The original flavour was chicken, I think, although I suspect that it was more flavouring than real chicken. Interestingly, when they were first marketed, the noodle packets were originally considered a luxury item with a high price, although year-on-year the price

THE OTHER SIDE OF HISTORY

reduced dramatically. After the demonstration and when everyone had left, Ando, who spoke no English, shook my hand and smiled some more. He gave me a packet of the noodles.

Later, Ando invented Cup Noodles — in 1971, I believe, when he must have been in his sixties — and that helped spark the popularity of the instant noodles craze overseas. He had noticed that Americans ate noodles by breaking the noodles in half, putting them into a cup and pouring hot water over them. They also ate them with a fork instead of chopsticks. Ando was inspired and felt that a Styrofoam cup, with a bottom narrower than the top, would be the ideal vessel for holding noodles and keeping them warm. Eating the noodles would then be as easy as opening the lid, adding hot water and waiting a minute or two.

Of course, Cup Noodles have now been copied everywhere round the world. It's one of those stories that come up at dinner parties. I like it. I liked him and I like his crazy quote that mankind is noodlekind.

THE LION IN LION CITY:

LEE KUAN YEW
COMES TO POWER

There was once a boy called David whose family lived in Muar, Johor, because his father worked as a clerk in a rubber plantation there. In the early 1930s, the world economy and especially the rubber price totally collapsed, putting David's father out of a job and throwing the family into crisis, forcing them to move back to Singapore. But the worst was yet to come. After a long series of difficulties in finding new jobs, his father committed suicide. David was only eight. The family had little money.

Thankfully, David had a kind uncle who sent him to study at the Anglo-Chinese School and then the Victoria School. But after an incident where he was accused (wrongly) of stealing a classmate's books, the 16-year-old David was forced to leave school. Unable to face his family, he decided to run away from home. To survive, he took up several odd jobs in restaurants and offices.

It was the early 1940s and the impact and horrors of the Second World War had reached Singapore. During the Japanese Occupation, in a twist of fate, David managed to master the Japanese language with the help of a friend who knew the basics and an English-Japanese dictionary. At the age of 18, he started working as an interpreter and translator to a high-ranking officer in the Japanese civilian police force.

After the war ended, David went to work as a clerk in the Public Works Department. In the early fifties, he pursued his studies and was enrolled at the University of Malaya, graduating in 1954. He then began what was to become a 40-year career in the civil service, taking on numerous roles at the Marine Department, Labour Research Unit, Ministry of Foreign Affairs and the Ministry of Defence.

David was working in the office of the Chief Minister of Singapore, Lim Yew Hock. But in the 1959 election, Lim Yew Hock's Singapore People's Alliance (SPA) was defeated by Lee Kuan Yew's People's Action Party (PAP). That caused Lim to step down as Chief Minister, and for Lee Kuan Yew to succeed him as the first Prime Minister of Singapore. David managed to stay on in key civil service roles and continued serving under Lee Kuan Yew, whom he admired greatly.

Singapore has always been an electrifying place. I really love it. I spent some time there in the late fifties. I was working at the famous

Raffles Hotel — which was at the hub of all the downtown action. I liked the buzz. And the people. A lot of political meetings were held at Raffles. It was central and there was an air of confidentiality about the place. I met David purely by chance the evening before the 1959 election results. He was meeting some foreign dignitaries along with a few politicians and he'd come out for a breath of air on one of the terraces. Other than him, there was only me.

I was a very humble, very junior house manager then, and I also had no clue who David was, since I only had a vague understanding of Singapore politics. Actually my knowledge was all but zero. I made to leave given that he was a guest, but he gestured that I should stay. He asked me about my job and enquired what I was doing away from my native country, America. We discussed Japan a little and both became quiet when, I believe, I mentioned Hiroshima. To change the subject, I asked David about his background. He told me a brief version of his story, much as I've told you — and we then discussed the current election. Was he concerned, I wondered, given that he'd been a big fish in the current administration? He didn't answer directly.

He said, "Prime Minister Lee Kuan Yew will be a most important political personality, of course. A third-generation, English-educated, Straits Chinese gentleman, Lee led his young PAP to its first victory in… 1955, supported surprisingly by both Communist and non-Communist elements. His goal was an independent, non-Communist, democratic socialist Singapore — once colonialism had been eliminated, of course. The key element in Lee's method was pragmatism rather than rigid ideology. He will be prime minister." Of this David was categorical and his face was firm in his belief.

Was he, I asked, so absolutely certain? Oh, wait, have you read *Ozymandias*? It's a sonnet written by the English poet Shelley, in the early 19th century. Oh, you know? 1818? OK. Good. Well, it's a great poem and it's relevant here. Hey, by the way, not that long ago archaeologists from Egypt and Germany found an eight-metre statue submerged in groundwater in a Cairo slum that they say probably depicts Pharaoh Ramses II, who ruled Egypt over 3,000 years ago. The pharaoh, also known as Ramses the Great or, get this, Ozymandias, was the third of the 19th dynasty of Egypt and ruled from 1279–1213 BC. I love that kind of thing, where suddenly we find historical relics. And I think that it's great that the discovery was made in the ordinary district of Matariya, among unfinished buildings and mud. The other side of history.

Anyway, I'd asked David how he could be so sure that Lee would become prime minister. David replied with a smile, "Ozymandias had a penchant for self-aggrandizing monuments. The boast etched in a plaque below his statue commanded lesser mortals to 'Look on my works'. Only the vastness of desert sands remains visible: no empire, no monuments, no great works. And the statue of Ozymandias lies half-buried in sand, wrecked and decayed." By alluding to *Ozymandias*, David was also cautioning against being overconfident. "I think," he said, "that Lee will remember that." He laughed and took a sip of his mint julep. He sat down while I, of course, remained standing. He indicated that I should sit. I looked around and did, but always on the edge of the chair.

"Up until recently," went on David, "he was known as Harry Lee, instead of using his given Chinese name Kuan Yew. It means Shining Light. His parents wanted their son to enter the professional classes or the colonial administration. After his Cambridge studies, returning to Singapore, Lee and his wife set up a law firm and he entered politics by campaigning for an end to British colonial rule. He gained political influence by advising union leaders on legal matters and helped form the pro-independence PAP in 1954.

"Well, Lee apparently judged (shrewdly as it turns out) that, as a member of the Straits Chinese elite, he had little chance of gaining power on his own, but his ability to harness the grassroots support of the trade unions might overcome that handicap. The PAP proved to be an uneasy alliance between mildly socialist politicians, such as Lee, and its pro-communist elements. Later, Lee cooperated closely with the British colonial Special Branch to keep the PAP militants under control."

David paused and looked at his watch. "Oh dear. Dear, oh

dear. I must go." And he put a hand on my shoulder and left. A kind man, I thought. An old one. A tired one.

Well... On the following day, May 30th it was, the national election results were released and PAP won 43 of the 51 seats in the legislative assembly. Singapore gained self-government with autonomy in all state matters except defence and foreign affairs — and Lee, at the age of 35, became the first Prime Minister of Singapore on June 3, 1959. Did pretty well, I reckon.

The founding prime minister of Singapore and a giant of post-war Asian history, Lee was fond of saying that his country never should have existed. "To begin with," he apparently said, "we don't have the ingredients of a nation, those elementary factors: a homogeneous population, common language, common culture and common destiny. So, history is a long time. I've done my bit."

He helped to transform his impoverished homeland into one of the world's most prosperous societies, a business and transportation hub that has enjoyed decades of peace, stability and economic growth. Lee's embrace of international trade — supported by the territory's strategic location along shipping lanes — turned Singapore into an attractive destination for foreign investment. And by insisting that all Singapore citizens adopt English as an official language, Lee helped foster a shared identity among the country's Chinese, Indian and Malay ethnicities.

"If it works, let's try it," he said in the interview with *The New York Times*. "If it's fine, let's continue it. If it doesn't work, toss it out, try another one."

THE AMERICAN DREAM:

JFK AND THE NEW RHETORIC

In the early sixties, I was in Washington D.C. and working in what is now The Willard InterContinental — a marvelous and historic hotel. I was a deputy manager by then. Often called the Crown Jewel of Pennsylvania Avenue, The Willard is conveniently located just one block away from the White House. Internationally known as one of the best hotels in Washington D.C., The Willard's blend of luxury, historic charm and hospitality subtly reflects the spirit of the city (at least that's what the brochures said!). But, seriously, it was a great hotel and I learned a lot there.

It was late March 1961, a couple of months after the United States had found itself a mercurial young president. Staying at the hotel was a kind, pleasant man called George St. John, the president's former headmaster at Choate School in Connecticut. He was a man of the church and his behaviour was charmingly old school.

It was a quiet Sunday afternoon and the good Reverend St. John was taking tea. He had asked me for a particular Sunday paper and I was pleased to go get it for him. He looked at the front page that was all about our new president. He tapped the paper and said, "This is a robust young man. The first Catholic to be entrusted with the presidency and, at 43, the youngest ever elected. A good man, but one who must acknowledge others." He had a twinkle in his eye. "Do sit for a moment if you are allowed." I said, "Well, I'm not really allowed, sir, but I will for a moment or two. Would you care for more tea?" He shook his head.

"As has often been said," went on George St. John, "the youth who loves his alma mater will always ask not 'what can she do for me?' but 'what can I do for her?'"

I replied, "That was in the president's inauguration speech, I believe?"

"Indeed it was," said the reverend, "and it was also in a number of mine too."

"I see, sir… Does that annoy you?"

"Not really, no. Well," he paused for a moment and sipped some tea. "It annoys some of my ex-pupils who knew Jack, and I believe that some of my colleagues find it highly irksome, but I think, no — I hope, that it's out of fondness and respect that he chose the phrase. Mark my words, son, this was an extraordinary speech. Brilliant, in fact. Rhetoric at its perfect best. Jack's 14-minute address was marked by sparkling phrase-making, including some special ones. May I repeat some to you?"

I was hardly going to say no. I nodded and smiled.

"Well, there's 'Let every nation know, whether it wishes us well or ill, that we shall pay any price, bear any burden, meet any hardship, support any friend, oppose any foe in order to assure the survival and the success of liberty.' Good huh? And then there's 'If a free society cannot help the many who are poor, it cannot save the few who are rich.' And, 'So let us begin anew, remembering on both sides that civility is not a sign of weakness and sincerity is always subject to proof.'"

I thought for a moment and said. "There was another, sir, I believe: 'Let us never negotiate out of fear, but let us never fear to negotiate.' Why do you have such an interest, may I ask?" The Reverend George paused for a moment.

"Where did you go to school, young man?" I told him. "Did you like it?" I said that, in the main, I had, which was more or less so. He didn't ask why I hadn't gone on after the age of 16 and I didn't volunteer anything.

"Well… the phrase: 'And so, my fellow Americans — ask not what your country can do for you, ask what you can do for your country.' This was what we all heard said to the whole Choate family," chuckled the good Reverend George.

"I'm sorry?"

"Choate School. I had the honour to be headmaster there. Jack Kennedy attended. Not necessarily the best pupil I have ever entertained, but nonetheless he has done well. They are saying that young Kennedy had resorted to underhand tactics. Nonsense, of course. I met Kennedy's eloquent speechwriter Ted Sorensen. John F. Kennedy's inaugural address was a joint effort with Ted. Ted and Jack are a great team. Wonderful minds and poets with language. Positioned the 'Ask not' piece brilliantly."

"Sir, I read that Mr. Sorensen credits the rousing call to arms of Abraham Lincoln and Winston Churchill as inspiration for JFK's inaugural address."

"Well, son, I'm sure that I don't figure in such company and I'm also certain that I figure small in our president's thinking. Sorenson writes with soaring rhetoric, but I suspect too that Mr. Sorenson will never take credit for the president's timeless phrases. That's as it should be of course. I am not an expert, but I would imagine that this speech will be rivalled only by Abraham Lincoln's inauguration — marked by similar sparkling phrase-making. Proclamations like, 'The torch has been passed to a new generation of Americans' is superb, and challenges citizens, as does, 'Ask not what your country can do for you, ask what you can do for your country.' Sorensen draws on the Bible, the Gettysburg Address and the words of Thomas Jefferson and Winston Churchill as he helped hone and polish that speech. Well, that's OK. That's OK."

"Sir, it has been a pleasure to meet you but I really must go. Duty calls. If there's anything you need, please let me know. Are you in town for business or pleasure?"

"Well, duty is an important calling. I'm in town for business I guess — and pleasure certainly. I'm to meet Jack tomorrow and he will want to know what I thought of his speech."

Memphis,
April 1968

A BLACK DAY:

THE ASSASSINATION OF MARTIN LUTHER KING JR.

Back to Memphis again. Told you so. It was early April in 1968. April 4, to be precise. I was, what, in my thirties and now the Executive Meetings Manager at the Peabody, that grand hotel in Memphis. Yes, I'd come back. I loved that job and that hotel. In those days, there weren't so many business meetings or corporate events as there are now — very few, in fact. Some board meetings, a few gatherings of suits, that kind of thing. Maybe the occasional Tennessee shoe manufacturers' conference or something, and sometimes a lodge meeting or a music industry awards ceremony. Actually, most events and meetings then *were* for the music business. I liked it there. The money wasn't great, but I liked the people. Memphis had become something of a hotspot for musicians and rock 'n' roll. Elvis of course.

I told you about the ducks. Remember the ducks? Well, it was 1933 when ducks were originally placed in the hotel's lobby fountain, setting up an 80 year tradition that continues today with the March of the Peabody Ducks. I love it. Well, the Peabody name has become synonymous with the North American mallard ducks that are now the living symbol of the Peabody brand. I do like that kind of thing.

The company that brought The Peabody back to life when they purchased the hotel was Belz Enterprises — a very good, highly successful, multifaceted real estate development and management firm based in Memphis. Anyway, April 1968. So, there was Memphis. There was Elvis. There were race riots: a police officer used his nightstick on a boy reportedly involved in the looting that followed the break up of a march led by Dr. Martin Luther King Jr. National guardsmen fixed bayonets to block civil rights activists trying to stage a protest on Beale Street. Marching demonstrators, wearing signs that read "I Am A Man", were also flanked by tanks! Tanks, for Chrissake. That made me so angry. It was a time of chaos in many ways, I guess. There was a student revolution in Paris. Russia was about to invade Czechoslovakia. Vietnam was in full bloody flood. Bobby Kennedy was to die later in the year. The starving Biafran population shocked an already shocked world...

I had been asked by my boss — Evernson was his name, Dick Evernson, an OK guy, always helpful to me... I still receive Christmas cards from his widow — well, he'd asked me to go over to the Lorraine Motel, only about half a mile away, to find a music manager and band leader who was staying there. There were some instruments that needed collecting from the Peabody and it was important that the music man should know that they'd arrived. Not my job, but it kind of was — I was in charge of staging musical events at the Peabody and I knew the music man. Anyway, Mr. Evernson thought it would be a nice and positive gesture. I thought so too. Anyway, so I went over with my message. I do recall that there'd been a garbage strike in Memphis and there was an unpleasant smell in the air.

The motel was full of important people who supported Dr. King. Let me tell you about that motel. The Lorraine was on 450 Mulberry Street and opened its doors in the mid-twenties. It had 16 rooms and stood just east of the Mississippi River. It was first named The Windsor and then later The Marquette. Then, in 1945, Walter and Loree Bailey (sweet people whom I met several times) bought it and called it after Loree, as well as after the popular song *Sweet Lorraine*. Well, the couple expanded the hotel by adding more guest rooms and a drive-up access, transforming it into a motel. It was a modest place, but clean and honest. Under the Baileys' ownership, the motel became a safe haven for black travellers and visitors to Memphis. Afro-American songwriters and musicians would stay at the Lorraine while they were recording in Memphis. Let's see — Ray Charles, Otis Redding, Count Basie, Aretha Franklin, Louis Armstrong, Sarah Vaughan and Nat King Cole were all guests. Two famous songs, *In the Midnight Hour* and

Knock on Wood, were written at the motel.

As I went in that day, I could find nobody to ask about my music man, the bandleader. Someone asked if they could assist me. It was Andrew Young. I had no clue then who the hell Andrew Young was. I can see that you don't know either. Well, he was one of Dr. King's closest friends and aides. He'd been involved in the civil rights movement for some years and had vociferously encouraged African Americans to register to vote and he sometimes faced death threats while doing so. That day, April 4, 1968, he'd been in a Memphis court fighting an injunction so that the Southern Christian Leadership Conference could help organise a second garbage workers' march; unfortunately, the first had ended violently. As I was talking to Mr. Young, Dr. King came downstairs and playfully chastised Young for not calling to let him, King, know of his whereabouts or something like that. But it was all smiles and friendly joshing. They also chatted about the court case. I sat down in the lobby to wait for the person to whom I was meant to give my message.

Then, down the stairs came another man, a Reverend Jesse Jackson, yeah — you've heard of him right? He'd spent the day helping to plan the SCLC's activities in Washington. He also brought down a bandleader affiliated with Operation Breadbasket, a community-organizing arm of SCLC that Jackson was running. He had rehearsed freedom songs with the band in his motel room. And it was this bandleader whom I was meant to meet.

As I say, Dr. King was bouncing about, laughing, kidding

around with everyone. He even came over to me and shook my hand. An open face and a great warmth in his smile. I knew who he was, of course. Everyone did. The atmosphere was a happy one. The bandleader was laughing with King and King was joking with his friends. I don't know why they stayed in the lobby, but it seemed to be the centre of the party. Walter Bailey, the motel's owner, didn't mind and, anyway, I was curious to know a bit more of this great orator and leader about whom I'd heard so much.

At around 5:45 p.m. King and some of his friends went upstairs and I got up to go. The bandleader walked me to the door and offered me five dollars for bringing over the message. I wasn't allowed to accept tips, so I refused but thanked him. I began to walk back to the Peabody not in any particular hurry.

Then just as I'd gotten some yards away, bang, a single shot. Bang. That was all. Bang. Not even a loud bang. But still, bang. Time stood still — it truly did — and then time moved on. Well, the rest I suspect you already know… More or less… The Reverend Doctor Martin Luther King Junior, standing on the second floor balcony of room 306 at the Lorraine Motel, was struck by a bullet at 6:01 p.m. on that day. He had stepped onto the balcony and was talking to friends who were in the parking lot below, still joshing, messing about and joking. He had just asked the saxophonist Ben Branch to play *Take My Hand, Precious Lord* at the rally that evening. As he turned to walk back into his room, a bullet hit him… and… that was it. Bang.

Well, the police in Memphis were put on alert for a "well-dressed" white man who was said to have dropped an automatic rifle after the shooting and escaped in a blue sedan car. There were early signs of rioting in Memphis that day and 4,000 National Guardsmen were drafted into the city. I remember that a dusk-to-dawn curfew was ordered. The President, Lyndon B. Johnson, postponed a trip to Hawaii for peace talks on Vietnam and spoke on TV about the killing of Dr. King.

King was the Lorraine Motel's most famous guest. He stayed at the motel numerous times while visiting the city. They say that poor Loree Bailey suffered a stroke when she heard the shot fired. She died on April 9, the same day as King's funeral. Something died in her husband's heart too. The motel, the site of the assassination, became dilapidated and by 1982, it was under foreclosure until a group of local citizens organised themselves, purchased the property and reopened it as a shrine to the nation's civil rights movement in 1991. I put in a little money.

Well now, King's helpers have gone in a variety of directions. Jesse Jackson returned to Chicago to expand his Operation Breadbasket into the Rainbow/PUSH Coalition; he also ran for president twice. Young became a U.S. Congressman, Mayor of Atlanta and a UN Ambassador. You know something? I met Jesse Jackson years later and, while he didn't remember me at all even though he was polite enough to say that he did, I asked him what he would say to Dr. King if he had the chance to speak to him again. "I guess the first report I would give to him is this: Dr. King, sir, I have not stopped working on your agenda, *the* agenda, since we last talked. I have *not* stopped." Jackson looked at the floor for a moment and I said nothing. He was chewing his lip. "I think", he said eventually, "that he would look at the accomplishments we've made and would probably say, 'Well done, but don't give up the battle. It's not over.'" Jackson paused and looked off across the hotel room in which we were standing. "And it ain't. Y'know," he said quietly, "he had just bent over the balcony rail a little. I reckon if he had been standing up he would not have been hit in the face."

I asked him about James Earl Ray. He sighed. "The assassination continues to bewilder people, even today," Jackson said. "One of the disturbing features about that day for us was that when we were pointing at where we thought the shot had been fired from, we were pointing over across the street. You recall? There was a building there, but there was also a six-to-eight-foot pile of bushes and some people thought that the shot came from the bushes. The FBI said it came from a bathroom window. When we got up the next morning, those bushes were gone."

Walter Bailey continued to run the motel, but he never ever rented Room 306 again. He turned it into a memorial. The room has now been preserved to capture exactly what it looked like on that tragic night. There are two beds — King was sharing the room with Dr. Ralph Abernathy, a friend. King's bed was not fully made because he had been a little tired — and had been lying down on the top.

In 1982, Walter Bailey declared bankruptcy and stood by

helplessly as his high-end establishment became a brothel. As I said, the property was sold in order to keep it as a shrine, I guess. The Lorraine Motel still stands on Mulberry Street. It's instantly recognisable and appears as though suspended in another time. Two large cars — a white 1959 Dodge Royal with lime green fins, and a white 1968 Cadillac — are parked in front of the motel. The motel sign features "Lorraine" printed on one side in a dramatic script against a bright yellow background and "Motel" is written on the other in large red block letters, each letter stamped inside its own white circle. A large white wreath hangs on the balcony outside Room 306, to mark the spot where King stood at the time of the assassination. Standing in front of the motel transports visitors to a bygone era. If you close your eyes, the iconic photograph of King's friends pointing off into the distance, at the place from which they believed the shot was fired, comes into sharp view. Walter Bailey died in July 1988, just over a year after the motel closed.

The immediate impact of the death of Dr. King was tragically played out, as angry Americans took to the streets, rioting in over a hundred cities round the country. You will recall from what I've told you already — and anyway you know — that this was a time when black people couldn't even sit next to whites on buses, when the races were rigorously kept apart in schools and when black Americans who spoke out against the indignities of racism were attacked and sometimes even lynched. In the 20th century. Oh indeed you may well say "oh…"

Earlier on the day he was killed, Dr. King had given a sermon

and in it he had said, "And he's allowed me to go up to the mountain and I've looked over and I've seen the Promised Land. I may not get there with you. But I want you to know tonight that we as a people will get to the Promised Land." I don't know if that's indeed precisely what he did say, but I like to think that it was.

I visited Memphis some years ago. I stood outside what was the motel. I wanted to go in, but I didn't... Nope, I didn't... As visitors exited the museum, I could see that they were looking at their shadows cast against a wall of silhouetted marchers...

London,
January 1969

ALL YOU NEED IS LOVE:

THE BEATLES BREAK UP

Set on Regent Street with rooms overlooking Piccadilly Circus, the Hotel Café Royal can't be beaten on location or on luxury. Inside the 1865 building lives a hotel of many parts, with what I believe are new intriguing spaces to explore around every corner. If you miss the main entrance, you can come into the hotel via The Café, a golden swirling marble room full of people eating wondrous cakes. Cakes always seem to taste better in places like this. They are small and tempting in every way — the marzipan, the chocolate, the cream. Sure, take one — these are good too. Each room of the hotel has a different theme and decor. There's the Green Bar which has its emphasis on absinthe reflected in the green-tiled walls and cocktails. And then there's the highly ornate

Oscar Wilde Bar — yes, he visited often — all gold gilding and red velvet, where you can watch cabaret in the evenings. It feels very like old world Paris. Which of course is the idea. However, in comparison, the upstairs of the hotel was more recently redesigned to have clean lines and clever lighting — minimalist. The rooms are spacious, with luxurious bits and pieces, and equipped with all the modern technology you'd expect. Or want. What gives the Café Royal a special edge is the view over real London. Relax in a leather armchair and just watch the city below. Love it.

Well, I liked The Beatles very much. There is a magic about them and this was one of the bands where every single track that they produced was different. The break up was such a sad thing. It was formally in April 1970, but the catalyst I think was a year before. I was working for a short time at the Café Royal in London in early 1969. I was having a ball. Rock 'n' roll. London. Music. Partying. Flower power. The Café Royal was and is famous for Wilde, as I've said and also many of the greats: Muhammad Ali, Winston Churchill, David Bowie, Albert Adrià and many other names. The place was sometime described as "the vibrant living room of London", the place to convene, converse and celebrate.

It was late and there were few diners left. There was one large party where people had begun to leave, but there was one guest lingering behind, with what looked like his bodyguard. Ringo Starr was sitting and looking down at the tablecloth. I approached and asked if he wanted anything else. We would never dreamed of asking anyone to leave. He asked for a soft drink, then wondered if

I'd heard about the roof concert that happened during lunchtime. I had, but not in much detail. He gulped his drink, went to the door and was collected by a chauffeur. The bodyguard stayed. He asked if he could have a strong coffee before he left and invited me to join him. So I did.

"The breakup really began in '67 with the death of Brian Epstein," said the man. Geoff was his name. Geoff something — I don't recall. "Brian was the one who kept the boys working together, resolving disputes, soothing bruised egos and, most importantly, handling the money. After he died, Paul tried to step into that role and act as group leader, but it didn't go down that well. Paul's first decision was to involve the group in the film *Magical Mystery Tour*. While the album did well, the film was a bloody disaster — awful in every way. John mocked Paul for its failure and, while Paul still ostensibly led the group, none of the band paid much attention to him.

"The boys began moving in different directions. John became more interested in the avant-garde art scene. At an exhibition in London, he met Yoko. They became an item and planned art projects together. In the beginning, John tried to get the rest of the group to join in, but they didn't fancy it. So, eventually John worked with Yoko on their artwork independently. At the same time, George was fed up. Really fed up. He felt that he was just as good a songwriter as either John or Paul, but the fact that he was only allowed two songs per album relegated him to a supporting role. So, he began working on solo projects — including the 1968 album, *Wonderwall*.

"Things really began to go downhill after the start of Apple Corps. Apple was a tax thing — if the guys didn't spend a lot of their income on what were called 'significant ventures', the government would hit them for more taxes. But Apple just leaked money. It was like a sieve. And running the business was a nightmare. None of the Beatles were businessmen. I think people knicked stuff — TVs, money, furniture, anything. If it wasn't nailed down, it went. The guys got ripped off. They needed a manager. John, George and Ringo wanted Allan Klein. Paul didn't trust Klein much and wanted to hire his father-in-law, Lee Eastman. Paul was outvoted and Klein was set two tasks: fix Apple Corps and turn the band's latest recording project into a profitable hit.

"The recording sessions for what would become *Let It Be* had been a disaster — everyone was arguing about everything — which songs to include, who should sing what, which support musicians to include, how to arrange the songs, who had the coolest clothes. When John brought Yoko in to the studio to work on songs and insisted that she be treated as an equal, the others were really pissed off, and John and Yoko got the cold shoulder for the rest of the sessions. Well, today man, they all tried to get it together."

The man paused and looked at his watch. "Better be going I reckon… They planned on performing live during the *Get Back* sessions earlier this month. George brought in keyboardist Billy Preston. Thought he'd help them to be tight and focused. There was a plan to play live somewhere. They were wondering where they could go — overseas or a huge venue somewhere. But that would have meant a big deal with kit and flights and people and stuff. So they decided to simply get up on the roof. At the end of *Get Back,* John said, 'I'd like to say thank you on behalf of the group and ourselves and I hope we've passed the audition.' Thanks for the coffee — and dinner was great. See you around, man."

I followed the break up of this super group. Paul was incensed that Klein had hired Phil Spector to work on the *Get Back* album tapes and accused Spector of ruining his songs. John was furious that his song *Cold Turkey* had been dropped from the *Abbey Road* album and recorded it on his own as a protest, crediting the writing to Lennon and not Lennon/McCartney. That'd never happened before. George was furious that Apple Corps was falling apart — and that he still wasn't going to be allowed more than two songs per album.

In April 1970, Paul released his *McCartney* album despite Klein's demands that it should wait until *Let It Be* was out. Three days later, Paul gave an interview in which he stated that he never wanted to work with any of the other three ever again. The other three all said everything was cool. In December 1970, Paul sued the other three Beatles for dissolution of the partnership and talk of another Beatles album ended. A dismal way to end. Some ends are dismal and some comfortable, don't you think? This, more than many, stuck in many minds as dismal — and while individual careers flourished, it was never really the same. Why would it be?

The story of The Beatles was always in some ways bigger than the group itself, I think. This was the story of a time, of a generation reaching out for new opportunities and possibilities. It was the story of what happens when you get there and achieve those opportunities and it was a story of what happens when it all falls totally to bits. It's a story of a romance that in the end the four guys just couldn't manage.

Catskill Mountains,
July 1969

LIGHT SIDE
OF THE MOON:

THE FIRST MOON
LANDING

I like to think that we all play a part, advertently or inadvertently, in history. Well, we undoubtedly do. Let me read something to you. On May 25, 1961, President John F. Kennedy spoke to Congress and famously said, "I believe that this nation should commit itself to achieving the goal, before this decade is out, of landing a man on the Moon and returning him safely to Earth. No single space project in this period will be more impressive to mankind or more important in the long-range exploration of space; and none will be so difficult or expensive to accomplish." Well, at the time I think he had absolutely no idea whatsoever if it could be done or, if it could, then whether it could be done by the end of the decade.

In 1969, I was working in New York State — the Catskill Mountains. Beautiful, green hills and valleys, waterfalls and lakes. Haven't been there in an age and I suppose that it's all a little overbuilt, overdeveloped these days. Anyway, I had one of my first deep love affairs there back in '69. Oh I know I shouldn't tell you, but I guess it doesn't matter now. The Catskills were where many upper middle class folks left in the summer for the cooler parts of the state. The summer vacation. The husbands would usually stay in town, in New York, and join their families at the weekends. Many kids were sent to camp in the Catskills. Some places encouraged mothers to be with kids. The mothers entertained themselves during the day and the kids "did" camp. Some families took off to the Catskills for a couple of months. I enjoyed my time there and the customers were demanding, yes, but always left huge tips if you did things right — and if you made a fuss of their kids. Which I did. Even the terrible ones. Many of the mothers were a bit bored I think. But I had a ball. And I fell in love. Or lust.

There were lots of new things happening at that time in the world: the first Led Zeppelin album came out and later in the year another, *Led Zeppelin II*. They still stand the test of time. Nixon became president, The Beatles gave their last live performance from a roof as I've just told you — and later in the year photographer Iain Macmillan took their photo on a zebra crossing on Abbey Road in London. The Concorde took off for the first time commercially and there was that awful Chappaquiddick incident where Mary Jo Kopechne died in a submerged car driven by Ted Kennedy. There was the Woodstock Festival — my gosh — Country Joe and The Fish, The Who, Jimi Hendrix... All amazing and brand new.

But something special happened on July 16 that I will never forget, standing in a hotel bar, with a lady guest's arm round my waist, all of us watching the TV. Glued — albeit me feeling not a little nervous about the lady's arm, but relishing the thought of the lady. Far too much information — you're quite right. Apollo 11 with Neil Armstrong, Buzz Aldrin and Michael Collins onboard lifted off toward the first landing on the Moon. On July 20, in the same bar and now having confessed unwavering something to a married woman, we all watched Apollo 11 "The Eagle" landing on the lunar surface. An estimated 500 million people worldwide watched in awe as Neil Armstrong took his historic first steps on the Moon, the largest television audience for a live broadcast ever — at that time. Can you imagine that? 500 million. In those days, that was just super huge.

There was end-to-end news coverage with interviews, viewpoints, dramatic diagrams. One interview with a specialist in particular interested me over the following days with his clear explanations and pleasant demeanour. He wasn't smug or self-satisfied.

George Mueller was the career space engineer who doggedly helped fulfill President Kennedy's vision of sending an American astronaut to the moon and back before the end of the decade. Dr. Mueller wrote in *The New York Times* on July 21, 1969, the day after Neil Armstrong took his giant leap for mankind, "This day man's oldest dream is made a reality — this day the ancient bonds tying him to the Earth have been broken." Three days later, with the Apollo 11 astronauts safely returned, Dr. Mueller declared, "Today at 11:49 a.m. Houston time, in the middle of the Pacific Ocean, we conclusively proved that man is no longer bound to the limits of the planet on which for so long he has lived."

He met JFK's deadline for a Moon landing — and, by the way, beating the Soviet Union in the space race of the decade — by daringly revamping testing procedures and by consolidating control over separate NASA centres in Alabama, Florida and Texas. He also pushed for the Skylab space station to test telescopes and other instruments and the effects of weightlessness, and urged the development of a reusable space shuttle. Like so many of that age, he was a visionary.

Dr. Mueller saw the space engineering potential in not only getting to the Moon but maybe beyond, and he grasped the scientific value of what might be discovered there. He also performed a promotional role, publicising the application of those advances to public health and other everyday purposes. "The stimulus of the space program has already produced more new knowledge and innovations in all aspects of our lives than any previous endeavour, even including a major war," he wrote.

In 1971, Richard Nixon awarded Dr. Mueller the National Medal of Science for "his many individual contributions" to the Apollo system. And John Logsdon, professor emeritus at The George Washington University's Space Policy Institute, said in an email, "Without his tough-minded management of the Apollo program, it is doubtful that NASA could have achieved President Kennedy's goal of a lunar landing before this decade was out."

Mueller was born in St. Louis in 1918. His father, Edwin, became an electrician and superintendent of a motor repair shop. His mother was a secretary. He had a boyhood keenness for model airplanes — you used to build those, didn't you? Well, George was keen. And model planes pointed him in the direction of aeronautical engineering, but the subject wasn't taught at the college his family could afford, the Missouri School of Mines and Metallurgy (now Missouri University of Science and Technology). So, he enrolled in mechanical engineering, then switched to electrical engineering and graduated in 1939. He received a master's degree from Purdue University, worked on microwave tubes, television and radar at Bell Laboratories and taught at Ohio State University while completing his doctorate in physics. Clever guy. He was vice president of Space Technology Laboratories in Los Angeles and while there he was hired by James Webb, NASA's key administrator, to lead the Apollo and Gemini initiatives through the Manned Spacecraft Center in Houston (now the Johnson Space Center),

the Marshall Space Flight Center in Huntsville, Alabama and the Kennedy Space Center in Florida. Not bad?

Dr. Mueller's reputation was so rock solid that he survived the repercussions from an explosive fire that killed three astronauts in their spacecraft on a launch pad in 1967. He was also able to persuade the rocket inventor Wernher von Braun to embrace an expedited "all-up" testing of a completed spacecraft instead of a more prolonged process of testing individual components and rocket stages one by one. Before Dr. Mueller launched Apollo 8 to orbit the moon in 1968, the rocket that lifted it into space had flown only twice. That doesn't sound like shocking news to you now maybe, but it sure was shocking news back then. But it shows what faith people had in this guy.

"I spent about four months that summer looking at every possible way that it could fail and convinced myself that it wasn't going to fail," he told the Smithsonian Institution's *Air & Space* magazine in 2011. "Yet too many people involved in spaceflight believe in trying to achieve absolute safety," he said. "If you designed your program to be absolutely safe, you'd also be sure you'd absolutely never fly." Well, I guess that there are those who would take a different view particularly when lives are at stake. But if you've ever read about other pushes by Man to explore what hasn't been explored, the risks are always high. Look at the sound barrier — Chuck Yeager was credited with being the first person to break the sound barrier in level flight on October 14, 1947 but in the process there were many casualties.

Dr. Mueller left NASA in December 1969 to return to private industry. He worked first at General Dynamics, then farmed jojoba shrubs as a substitute for sperm whale oil, which is used as a lubricant — and still later joined Kistler Aerospace Corporation. In a 1998 oral history transcript about NASA, he said, "It's clear that you have a limited time of effectiveness in Washington, if you really are doing anything. If you're not doing anything, you can stay there indefinitely. That's it."

ENTER BILL GATES
AND PAUL ALLEN:

THE FIRST REAL
HOME COMPUTER

New York is still one of my very favourite cities. Yours too I guess? Venice as well? OK. Yes I can understand that. But let's see... I have many favourites — Venice, sure, New York, of course, Sydney, Budapest, London, Berlin, Memphis, Albuquerque... amongst many others. So many favourites! Many are associated with people and good times, of course — as well as beauty. Well, in 1975, I was working in Albuquerque, New Mexico and the place was just buzzing.

I was working hard. Always did. There was a meeting in the hotel — a *Popular Electronics* magazine meeting. No big deal really because there were always meetings going on in the hotel. I met the editor, Arthur Salsberg, at the reception and showed him to his meeting room. I was asked to stay. Why? Well, I knew shorthand and their secretary for the day was unwell. Why did I know shorthand? Because I was always looking for extra skills to learn. I wasn't great at shorthand and of course who uses it now? Exactly.

Art Salsberg was the new editor of *Popular Electronics* and he was a worried guy. The magazine's arch-rival, *Radio-Electronics*, was gaining readers and he needed to head off the challenge big time. It was all a bit dog eat dog back then. He consulted Leslie Solomon, his technology editor, who had an idea for a cover story for the January 1975 issue. The story was this: MITS — I think it stood for Micro Instrumentation and Telemetry Systems — a company based in Albuquerque, was apparently producing a cheap, powerful mini-computer in kit form. Nothing like these things we use now. The business had made a lot of money producing electronic calculators. They wanted a new product. Well, Salsburg and Solomon were to meet some of the people from MITS that day at my hotel. I had no real clue what was being discussed.

Apparently, Ed Roberts, the founder of MITS, had produced a number of kit calculators over the years, but now the company was stepping things up a gear. The parts list was long and complex, with disc capacitors, resistors, LEDs, switches, a new 2MHz Intel chip and God knows what else. Roberts built a prototype and sent it to Solomon — but apparently it got lost in the post, so the article had been drafted ready to print with reference to pictures and diagrams and the cover illustrated using an empty box with flashing lights.

According to the meeting, the computer still hadn't got a name just before the article had been printed. "Why don't you call it Altair?" apparently suggested Solomon's 12-year-old daughter, Lauren, who had been watching Star Trek. "That's where the Enterprise is going tonight." Well, so the story goes. I like these "what happened at the beginning" tales. They have charm, don't you think? Apple for instance. On the naming of Apple, Jobs apparently said that he was "on one of my fruitarian diets." He said he had just come back from an apple farm and thought the name sounded "fun, spirited and not intimidating." Adobe was so called apparently because Adobe Creek ran behind founder John Warnock's house. Garmin was so called after founders Gary Burrell and Dr. Min Kao. Lego is from the Danish *leg godt*, which means to play well. Less appetizing is Pepsi, named from the digestive enzyme pesin. Starbucks is named after a character in Herman Melville's *Moby Dick*. And so on.

Anyways, back to the story… The January 1975 issue hit the stands in December 1974. "For many years," read the editorial, "we've been reading and hearing about how computers will one

day be a household item… What we're presenting to you, dear reader, is a mini-computer that will grow with your needs."

The Altair 8800 had no keyboard and no display; programming instructions were entered via switches on the front panel, with the results then displayed via LED lights. Yes, I know, not my strong suit. Roberts was expecting 800 orders at most, but he was overwhelmed; by August he had shipped 5,000 kits and hired dozens of new staff. "The number of customers has increased more rapidly than our ability to train," he wrote in October. Salsberg's editorial had boldly announced that "the home computer is here. Finally." He was right, more so than he could ever possibly know.

At the end of that meeting in Albuquerque, I handed my notes over to the team. I was thanked (although I was a tad concerned that my shorthand notation might have been less than solid) and I thought little more about it. By the way, always get yourself a skill — anything — aside of your career. You never, ever know when it'll come in handy. Sure, guitar is good.

Ed Roberts was saying his goodbyes and see-you-soons to people from the meeting. A young guy came up to me and said, "Excuse me sir, but is that Ed Roberts?" I replied that it was. He thanked me and he asked if he might meet Mr. Roberts. I said that this wasn't up to me. As coincidence would have it (and coincidence very often does have it, I find), Ed Roberts was just passing by then and the young man, now joined by another fresh-faced hopeful, excused themselves from me and asked Mr. Roberts if he had 10 minutes to listen to an idea concerning the Altair.

Roberts said "sure" and the two guys introduced themselves...
Paul Allen and Bill Gates.

Microsoft was founded in Albuquerque, New Mexico, on April 4, 1975 by Bill and Paul. It was set up to develop and sell BASIC interpreters for the Altair 8800. You know much of the rest I guess. The youngsters moved to Albuquerque to work for MITS and in July 1975 left to start Microsoft.

THE GREAT DICTATOR:

THE RISE AND RISE OF SADDAM HUSSEIN

Let me tell you a story. Yes, yes, I know... But another kind.

Imagine Baghdad, but not as it is today. In 1534, Baghdad was conquered by the Ottoman Turks. Under the Ottomans, Baghdad fell into a period of decline, partially as a result of the enmity between its rulers and Persia. For a time, Baghdad had been the largest city in what is now called the Middle East before being overtaken by Constantinople in the 16th century. The city remained under Ottoman rule until the establishment of the Kingdom of Iraq under British control in 1921. Iraq was given formal independence in 1932. The city's population grew from an estimated 145,000 in 1900 to 580,000 in 1950 of which, interestingly, 140,000 were Jewish. During the 1970s Baghdad experienced a period of prosperity and growth because of a sharp increase in the price of oil, Iraq's main export.

In Iraq, all roads lead to the capital Baghdad, the City of the Caliphs and birthplace of Sinbad, the famous sailor and prosperous merchant. Sure you did, that's right. It's a city with a glorious past. Modern Iraq occupies the territory that was the old Mesopotamia, populated by ancient Sumerians, Babylonians, Assyrians, and was also the site of the glorious sun-burst of the Abbasid Empire of Harun al-Rashid. It's the Persia of old stories and is the centre of much that is mentioned in the Bible, including the Garden of Eden. In other words, 1970s Baghdad was the heart of a former cradle of civilization, a country as historically dramatic as the Nile Valley or Ancient Greece.

Baghdad, as a name, had been mentioned as Baghdadu on the 9th century BC Assyrian cuneiform records and the 6th century BC Babylonian bricks bearing the Royal Seal of King Nebuchadnezzar found in the Tigris. It also appeared in many other historical records prior to the Christian era. The name Baghdad is probably a combination of two Persian words meaning "founded by God". Locals called it Dar Essalam, "the City of Peace". Well, it was, back then.

Imagine the 16th century and the city's centre — with the caliph's palace and the grand mosque with four roads radiating out from these central buildings. Imagine a city that has expanded beyond its original walls and spread across to the river's east bank, its two halves joined by a bridge built of boats. The eastern section was called Rusafa and the western section was called Karkh. The river's wharves were lined with ships — from China bringing porcelain, from Malaya and India with spices and dyes, from Turkestan with lapis lazuli and slaves, from East Africa with ivory and gold dust and from Arabia with pearls and weapons.

Mathematics was developed in Baghdad. It was a place of learning and commerce. Aristotle and Plato were translated. Caliph Mamun built an astronomical observatory where savants measured the Earth's surface 600 years before Europe admitted that it wasn't flat. In the 1970s there was a mix of colours, races, costumes and ways of life. The city had an air of vitality and excitement.

In Rusafa, the eastern part of the city, is Al-Rashid Street, the city's main street, stretching from North Gate to South Gate. In the seventies it was still very much the commercial centre of Baghdad. There were and are many side streets and alleyways. Let's imagine that it's the end of a hot July day with temperatures approaching 48 degrees. The man in the very dirty, stained *thwab* edges forward along the alleyway in the dying light. In his left hand, he holds a large knife with a razor edge. In his right, an American revolver. He's going to seize his chance. You know, my boy, life and time are not straight lines. I've said that before. It's true. Nothing is safe: life and death often hinge on how often people venture out and how far they stray and at what time of day; which intersections and bridges they have to cross; which streets they negotiate and which form of transport they choose — private car, taxi or on foot. Bear with me... The man who'd been wearing filthy clothes, with the knife and a gun, had already disposed of the bloody knife and the clothes and was now smartly dressed in army uniform. He called a meeting of several hundred top party officials. This man, the new President of Iraq, said there had been a plot against him. Names were read out and the accused were promptly taken out of the hall one by one and shot. Dead.

Within days, a personality cult had grown around Saddam Hussein. They (whoever *they* were) said that he had a Quran written in his blood, an attempt to show he was directly descended from the prophet Muhammad. He was attributed to having written a romantic novel that was turned into a lavish musical. He had a film made of his youthful assassination attempt on Qasim. He was known, or wanted to be known, in Iraq as "Great Uncle" or "the Anointed One".

The hotel in which I worked then was in central Baghdad. The business doesn't own it anymore and to be honest I don't mind. I was hotel deputy manager for two hotels and was on duty. I was told that a top five-star general wanted to use the hotel for a number of government meetings — quite normal back then and the authorities never paid or, if they did, it was less than it should have been and always late. Bribery was rife. And woe betide us if one of Saddam's two terrible sons was involved. The general had requested a meeting and I arranged that. I had no choice of course. He was late and, when he did arrive, he asked his guards to wait outside the room. He sat down, accepted some mint tea, ate a small Swedish biscuit (a favourite of his and therefore provided), placed a large wad of pristine American dollars wrapped neatly in a clear plastic envelope on the table and spoke in excellent English.

"The president may wish to sleep at your hotel from time to time," he growled. "This," here he indicated the dollars, "guarantees that you tell nobody." The general paused and looked at me, tapping the wad of cash with a well-manicured fingernail. He appeared in no big hurry and I have to tell you that I was sweating and very nervous. I couldn't take the money of course — and it was a *lot* of money, all hundred dollar bills and I judged that the total would have been many, many thousand. "Let me tell you something about the president," said the general. "He was born in a village just outside Tikrit in April 1937. In his teenage years, Saddam immersed himself in the anti-British and anti-Western atmosphere of the day. At college in Baghdad, he joined the Ba'ath party and in 1956 he took part in an abortive coup attempt. He wanted to kill. He would often dress as a local beggar in filthy clothes, but he would be well-armed. And he would kill." The general paused to sip some tea and to take another biscuit. His manner was effete.

"After the overthrow of the monarchy two years later, my president plotted to kill Abd al-Karim Qasim, our then prime minister. But the conspiracy was discovered and Saddam had to leave the country." The general bit the end of the thin biscuit and examined what remained. I could hear muted noises from the outside world; it mixed comfortably with the gentle hum of the air conditioning. "In 1963," went on the general, "with the

Ba'ath party in control in Baghdad, the president returned home and began to find positions of influence. During this period he married his cousin Sajida. This shocks you? They later had two sons and three daughters. Wonderful children. But within months, the Ba'ath party had been overthrown and Saddam was jailed, remaining there until the party returned to power in a coup in July 1968." The general paused to eat another biscuit. He brushed crumbs from his sleeve.

"Saddam gained a position on the ruling Revolutionary Command Council. For years, he was the power behind the then sick president, Ahmed Hassan al-Bakr. In 1979, Saddam achieved his ambition of becoming head of state. The new presidency started as it intended, by doing good for Iraq and its people. You will think that he is cruel but, my friend, we have to show strength. Last week, everyone had to watch a video aired on the Iraqi television. You saw it?" This last was more of a assumption than a question and the general looked hard into my eyes. He paused. I just stared and tried not to blink. "The video," said the general slowly, "featured Saddam sitting onstage at the national theatre. He smokes a cigar. A plot leader confesses his crime. Then the man reads out the names of his supposed co-conspirators. Anyone named would be taken outside the theatre and immediately executed. Everyone inside could hear what was happening outside. Remaining members of the audience called out their allegiance to my president, trying not to look afraid. No one knows whose name is going to be called out next. This meant that the survivors cheer even more frenziedly for Saddam Hussein. It's very wonderful television. My president wanted that to be seen by everyone. Iraqí or not Iraqí. This was an exercise of power to impress upon the surviving Ba'athists in Iraq that he had absolute control over their lives — and their deaths."

The general stopped and stood up. He straightened his jacket and thanked me for the tea and the biscuits. I stood too. The general saluted, turned and left. I sat down again and with a shaking hand, rang my boss, an Iraqí through and through — a man who worked hard and ran a good hotel. He was at home with his family, but came over to see me straight away. Before he did anything he put the dollars in the hotel safe. Then he came back and sat me down for a chat.

"For some years now," he said, "every single move has had to be calculated. What happened today — well, we have to do what they want. I may end up in prison or worse. You are in less trouble — they wouldn't hurt an American — not yet anyway. Saddam's regime has developed a brutal tactic, which involves asking children about their parents' behaviour towards him and the regime. For example, would their parents keep watching the TV when Saddam was on screen or would they switch off or change channel? Many families were wiped out, because one of their children had said that they actually turned off the TV.

Cartoons, songs, textbooks, notebooks, colouring books, even homework assignments are all being dedicated to Saddam. It is a nightmare." And this normally even-handed, level-headed, clever man looked terrified. He went on, "The regime was always there from the start to shake everyone's world. Those who have power disrespect the law because only the weak and vulnerable respect it. Driving through the streets of Baghdad, I see a brand new sports car speeding at a hundred miles an hour, beating a red light. You know that a police officer wouldn't dare to issue a traffic ticket." He paused to wipe his face with his handkerchief.

So, Saddam made his move on his old patron, Al-Bakr, and forced his relative to resign and then took over the presidency himself. And he purged the party's Revolutionary Command Council. This was a one-man regime... And yes it was in the name of the Ba'ath Party and yes there was some kind of ideology, but the ideology was whatever Saddam said it was. He defended his autocratic style of leadership by arguing that nothing else could have kept such a vast and diverse nation united. The country pumped billions into the capital after it first struck oil, with substantial contributions from Europe. German engineers built Baghdad's freeways, the French its airport and the Scandinavians its hotels. The country oozed money.

Saddam rarely stayed in his own apartments, houses or government buildings — places like the Al-Faw Palace, the lakeside palace near Basra, the Republican Palace and all the heavily guarded houses. He visited family's houses for dinner and a bed or he'd go to hotels like ours back then for an overnight stay. Always heavily guarded. The Al Mansour Hotel, for example, had a permanent guard. As did the hotel I worked in.

You see things. You say nothing. My manager told me, "Look," he said earnestly, "Don't speak about this unless you absolutely must. Be careful. There will be foreign dignitaries. There will be spies everywhere. Saddam Hussein's playboy sons may come here again, with their entourage — remember how disgustingly rude to staff they are? They are animals and anyone who argues, well... We dread them and indeed any of the new government people. Like that general just now. And hotel staff are frightened — who knows who are the spies, staff or guests?" He stopped. "I could be a spy. Or you could." I tried to smile. "I'd make a terrible spy," I said weakly.

"Listen," said my manager with no smile on his face. "One evening, three men came into the hotel. They went straight to the desk. One was in uniform and the other two wore traditional dress. Everyone in the lobby stopped talking and looked anywhere but at the man who was smoking a cigar and looking round the reception area. By the hotel's front doors, there was a group of heavily armed soldiers. The man in uniform turned around and caught my eye. He held my gaze and then I had to look away. Instinctively, you don't feel that this is a loathsome person. He doesn't come across in that way. He seems almost kindly. But you can't get out of your mind what you know about his ruthlessness and the way that he does not care much for human life."

DEATH COMES KNOCKING:

INDIRA GANDHI'S ASSASSINATION

In the mid-eighties I was based in Delhi, in Maidens Hotel. The hotel is ideally located, only a mile or so away from the famous Mughal monuments and popular Indian bazaars. It was established in 1903 to host the attending dignitaries for the Delhi Durbar, held to celebrate the coronation of King Edward VII and Queen Alexandra as Emperor and Empress of India. On that occasion, they also laid the foundation stone for New Delhi, a new capital city located at the centre of North India, deemed to be more strategically placed than the capital then, which was Calcutta on the east coast. The architect, Sir Edwin Lutyens, unveiled a grand plan for an imperial garden city, which could be expanded in every direction — one worthy of the jewel in the crown of the British

Empire. Delhi, with New Delhi contained within, has since expanded to become a sprawling metropolis covering many districts... Ah yes, you did, didn't you... I do remember... a few years ago.

Well, back then, I was friendly with a few locals including a young Sikh trainee surgeon from a middle-class background, interested in rock 'n' roll, beer and cricket. The Punjab to the north was fractured by violence between Sikh militants and government forces. People like my friend, who argued that both sides were committing atrocities, were shouted down. He was frustrated and distressed, but life in Delhi carried on. All that changed at 9:20 a.m. on October 31, 1984... Boy did it change.

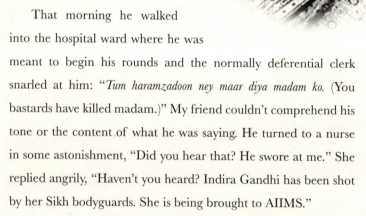

That morning he walked into the hospital ward where he was meant to begin his rounds and the normally deferential clerk snarled at him: "*Tum haramzadoon ney maar diya madam ko.* (You bastards have killed madam.)" My friend couldn't comprehend his tone or the content of what he was saying. He turned to a nurse in some astonishment, "Did you hear that? He swore at me." She replied angrily, "Haven't you heard? Indira Gandhi has been shot by her Sikh bodyguards. She is being brought to AIIMS."

The All India Institute of Medical Sciences was the big

neighbour to my Sikh friend's hospital and it was where the VIPs all went. The smaller hospital served the poor, the dispossessed and those without political or economic clout. My friend immediately rushed to AIIMS, which was already seething with people. Most spoke in hushed mutterings, the crowd swarmed anxiously, occasionally someone shouted, senior government figures arrived with blaring alarms, security guards were everywhere waving guns and batons. There was an ominous foreboding in the still, humid air.

A senior doctor who knew my friend approached him and whispered, "It's not safe for Sikhs. You should leave." The gates were blocked by teeming crowds. As my friend squeezed his way through, someone shouted, "You bastard!" and he was hit hard with something on the head. His turban came off. His head was bleeding and, clutching his turban, he forced his way through as more blows rained down upon his back. He managed to stumble into an auto-rickshaw, begging the driver to take him away and waving cash in the man's face. My friend wasn't badly hurt, just very badly shaken — and frightened. The blows he received were a manifestation of grief turned into anger. It was unfocused, not directed at him personally but at the Sikhs who were responsible for the death of Indira Gandhi, the country's mother. If that had been all, then it would have been kind of OK, but it wasn't all. Not by a long shot.

The killings started late that evening. National television had a continuous broadcast of footage of Indira Gandhi's body, surrounded by crowds shouting, "*Khoon ka badla khoon.* (Seek blood for blood.)" Rumours were rife. It was alleged that trains were arriving from Punjab where all the Hindu passengers had been killed by the Sikhs onboard. It was said that Sikhs were celebrating and distributing sweets. It was also said that Sikhs had poisoned the Delhi water supply.

Two police officers from my friend's local police station went around our area with a megaphone, shouting, "Don't drink the water. The Sikhs have poisoned it." My friend challenged them, "Do you think taps know the religion of a household? Would Delhi Sikhs be able to avoid being poisoned? What nonsense is this?" One of them pushed him aside with his rifle. The other spat at him. Our residential area had a large number of Sikh families and a dominant Hindu population. Elders from the Hindu and Sikh communities convened a meeting at the local temple. Our Hindu neighbours reassured my friend and his friends that they would protect them. Street patrols were formed and young people were placed on rooftops to look out for approaching mobs. It was very frightening. The Sikhs patrolled the area with whatever weapons they could find: hockey sticks, cricket bats, tennis rackets, axes, broomsticks. My friend's father had a ceremonial Sikh sword, four feet long, but it was blunt and useless. My friend walked around with it unsheathed, unsure whether he would have the nerve to ever use it. We could see fires raging in the distance. We heard that Sikhs were being killed in large numbers, but there was no way to find out the truth.

THE OTHER SIDE OF HISTORY

My friend and I sat in our hotel and there were anxious stares at him from time to time but nothing more. He told me that he had never before experienced what he then felt: a sense of being hunted. He was an enemy in his own country. Unbeknownst to him and actually to any of us, mobs had been formed by senior members of the ruling Congress Party. Electoral lists were distributed so that Sikh households could be identified. The mobs, already suffused with anger, were plied with alcohol, paid a thousand rupees each and given canisters of kerosene. The mob would surround a Sikh house and shout for all the males to step outside. The men would then have their legs broken before being doused with kerosene and set on fire, as the women and children watched. There was rape, there was looting but the primary aim of the mob was bloodlust — *"Khoon ka badla khoon..."* Terrible times. Terrible.

The violence continued for three days. About eight thousand Sikhs were killed in Northern India, with more than three thousand in Delhi. My friend was able to leave the area, hiding in the back of a Hindu friend's car. He went looking for a family we knew a few miles away, but the streets were deserted and the family had fled. He found a badly burnt girl; she was around 15 and barely alive. He tried to get her admitted to a local hospital but the A&E consultant refused to admit her. He found a relief camp and left her there. To this day, my friend doesn't know if she survived. Several thousand of the widows and children from the carnage were rehoused in what became known as the Widow Colony. The women were in a state of perpetual mourning, the children neglected and left to their own devices. All around they could see people who had killed their fathers, grandfathers, uncles and brothers; the killers safe in the knowledge that they were beyond the law. Beyond the law.

Even though I was advised not to, I started visiting the colony along with some friends, initially just to bring a few bits and pieces, to play with the children and to give them some comfort. We met in a playground in a park. But the children, terrified of strangers, wouldn't attend. So my friend offered to help provide free medical care to all families who would send the kids to the play area. Out went his surgical career, in came a weekly round of collecting medicines or money from friends like me and holding a makeshift clinic at weekends. I helped when I could.

He worked with those families for about two years. Every official inquiry exonerated the perpetrators, dismissing robust evidence on the flimsiest of grounds. My friend decided to become a psychiatrist and moved to Chandigarh, the capital of Punjab. Here the cycle of violence between the Sikh militants and the government continued. When my tour of duty in India finished and I left my hotel, I left a very different India and was both disheartened and ashamed. On the evening before I left Delhi, I was taken to see some hotel acquaintances at the Taj Mahal Hotel in Mansingh Road. Then I had dinner there with some friends. Simranjit Singh was there. He's a Sikh surgeon who suffered during that period over thirty years ago.

"1984 remains one of the darkest years in modern Indian

history," he said in a firm voice possibly just that little bit too loud. "In June of that year, Prime Minister Indira Gandhi ordered a military assault on the most significant religious centre for the Sikhs, Sri Darbar Sahib — the Golden Temple — in Amritsar, Punjab. The attack killed thousands of civilians. On October 31, 1984, as you know, she was assassinated by two of her Sikh bodyguards. You know that her assassination triggered genocidal killings around the country, particularly in New Delhi. Frenzied mobs of young Hindu thugs, thirsting for revenge, burned Sikh-owned stores to the ground, dragged Sikhs out of their homes, cars and trains, then clubbed them to death and/or setting them on fire before raging off in search of other victims.

"There is something truely terrible about mob frenzy. Witnesses watched in horror as the mobs walked the streets of New Delhi, gang-raping Sikh women, murdering Sikh men and burning down Sikh homes, businesses and gurdwaras (Sikh houses of worship). Eyewitness accounts describe how law enforcement and government officials participated in the massacres by engaging in the violence, inciting civilians to seek vengeance and providing the mobs with weapons. The pogroms continued unabated and, according to official reports, within three days nearly 3,000 Sikhs had been murdered. Unofficial death estimates were far higher and human rights activists identified specific individuals complicit in organizing and perpetrating the massacres." He did pause then for a short moment, when one of the other guests consulted him on a professional medical issue.

"Almost as many Sikhs died in a few days in India in 1984," he went on turning back to me, "as all the deaths and disappearances in, say, Chile during Pinochet's 17-year military rule. Those who survived the violence have yet to receive any semblance of justice. Most perpetrators have yet to be held accountable for their crimes and many of the affected families continue to live in poverty and disenfranchisement. The Indian government's formal position for three decades has been that accountability comes in the form of silence."

Well, it was a ghastly moment in India's history, though the Indian government was certainly not the first to massacre its own citizens. Many of the nations complicit in ethnic cleansing — Chile, Argentina, Rwanda and South Africa amongst others — eventually recognised, or began to recognise, the importance of addressing past atrocities. Yet the Indian state stubbornly refused and still refuses to admit its fault and take ownership of its participation in mass violence, despite enormous evidence to the contrary. The term commonly used to describe the anti-Sikh pogroms of 1984 is "riot". The word riot is problematic because it implies random acts of disorganised violence. It invokes images of chaos that overwhelms law enforcement and the government that is there to protect its own people. The anti-Sikh violence of 1984 was not a riot. The massacres were not spontaneous, anomalous or disorganised. As my surgeon companion at that dinner said, "Until this is addressed, political stability will remain a challenge as minorities in India, including its more than twenty million

Sikhs, will continue to feel alienated and targeted by their own government."

Let me tell you something — and think of this as you fly back to New York. I heard this from my medical friend, now a prominent psychiatrist in Chandigarh. A lady called Surinder Kaur was at her home in Delhi when the mob broke in. Diwali, the biggest festival of the season, had just ended, but she and her husband had left the lights around the house up. Why not? In just 15 days, their eldest son was getting married, and the celebrations were already getting under way. This was a happy family. Then a horde of more than two thousand people descended on their middle-class neighbourhood, killing dozens of Sikh families and burning alive Kaur's soon-to-be-married son and husband with petrol from the family's motorbike. They've never celebrated another festival since.

Cape Town,
February 1990

BORN FREE:

NELSON MANDELA'S RELEASE FROM PRISON

In 2011, I attended a special event in South Africa. I made a short speech, in fact. It was an event partly sponsored by our business and was all about education in the region, particularly for adults who couldn't read or write. Well, hell, we should do things like that. Ahmed Kathrada was a guest at the event in Jo'burg. He had been sentenced to life imprisonment at the Rivonia Trial. He was released in 1990. He and I talked. The trial was named after Rivonia, the suburb of Johannesburg where leaders had been arrested at Liliesleaf Farm, on July 11, 1963. The farm had been used as a hideout for the African National Congress and others. Nelson Mandela had moved onto the farm in October 1961 and evaded security police while masquerading as a gardener called

David Motsamayi, meaning "the walker". The leaders who were prosecuted in the Rivonia Trial also included Mandela, who was already in Johannesburg's Old Fort Prison serving a five-year sentence for inciting workers to strike and leaving the country illegally. Most of the Rivonia defendants were to be convicted and in turn sentenced to life imprisonment.

"In the first years," said Kathrada, "we were allowed one visit, one letter, every six months. And the letter had to be no more than 500 words. But we had colleagues who were illiterate. Mr. Mandela encouraged us all to study. Not only politics, but also learning to read and write. That type of initiative was very, very important. It also helped with morale. On Robben Island, the key activists led by example. When we were on hunger strikes they refused to be exempted — because we had taken a decision in the ANC that our senior people, particularly those who were old and not too well, should be exempted. But they refused. We knew that the families of Mandela and Walter Sisulu were being harassed by the police all the time — detained, children tortured, people sent into exile — but they never allowed their concern for their families overshadow their concern for their fellow prisoners.

"When somebody was at low ebb, you'd see Mr. Mandela or Mr. Sisulu going up to them, cheering them up. And Mr. Mandela himself, he was offered more leniencies than other prisoners. He refused, saying that he'd accept them only if they applied to everyone. If they were going to exempt him from work, then everybody should be exempt. Through his actions, he managed to instill into people the notion of equality and dignity. On Robben Island, we would never kowtow to the white wardens or do anything that violated anyone's integrity. When he challenged President de Klerk openly on a TV programme, chastising him right at the beginning of the negotiation, Soweto was dancing! Here was a black man talking to his so-called white superior as an equal. Yet he always emphasised that he was not a saint. He said that he was a human being, who had made errors just like anyone else.

"He also brought a sense of security to our white compatriots. Prior to 1994 there was widespread fear among whites that when the ANC came into power they were going to lose their houses, be driven into exile or killed. Among the first things Mr. Mandela did as president was invite the wives and widows of apartheid presidents and prime ministers and ministers to tea… and then there was the famous match in 1995, when South Africa hosted the Rugby World Cup. He stepped on to the field with all those Afrikaners there to congratulate our Afrikaner team. That must have taken courage. It was acts like these that encouraged white people to feel protected, so that the exodus was not as great as it could have been.

"Politicians can find it difficult to laugh at themselves. Not him. I remember him talking to a crowd. Soon after his release he was in the Transkei and a little girl confronted him. 'How old are you?' she asked. And you know he's very patient, so he took time to engage the child, so that she understood. She asked, 'I hear you were in prison. Why were you in prison?' And so he explained ... 'How long were you in prison?' and he explains again. So she kept on. Eventually she got frustrated and said, 'You are just a stupid old man!' And he related this to the crowd. He's able to laugh at himself without inhibitions; very few politicians are able to do that..."

I visited Robben Island... Oh not back then, but some time later. It's a low, scrubby oval, a few miles offshore, which can be made out from any of the heights around Cape Town. Mandela disappeared from the world for 27 years with the reputation of a charismatic but often boastful lawyer, a keen boxer and a ladies' man who did not have the temperament to remain undetected for long even when he went underground. I remember talking once to John McCarthy, the British journalist who was held hostage for five years in Lebanon. It is just impossible to imagine what these things can mean, or do, to a human being.

Mandela returned a dignified old man who had won the respect of his captors, so much so that they were anxious to negotiate the handover of power to him. Robben Island is now a World Heritage Site, but when visitors see the conditions in which he lived for so long, few find it easy to imagine how he retained his sanity, let alone how he triumphed over his oppression. The cell in which he spent his many years was barely six feet square.

Mandela recalled his first arrival on the island in his book *Long Walk to Freedom* — it's there, yes do take it, of course — let me just read something to you: "We were met by a group of burly white warders shouting in Afrikaans: '*Dis die Eiland! Hier gaan julle vrek!* (This is the Island! Here you will die!)'" Despite poor food, inadequate clothing in the wet and windswept Cape winter and heavy labour in the island's lime quarry, where Mandela's sight was damaged by the blinding glare of the sun on the quarry's blanched walls, he remained unbroken.

"The authorities' greatest mistake was to keep us together, for together our determination was reinforced," he wrote. The bullying, poorly educated white warders were uncertain how to deal with these articulate, determined political prisoners, who seemed confident that they would one day prevail, no matter how long their sentences were or how complete the white regime's apparent domination. By the early 1970s, Mandela had tamed the prison authorities to the point that they would frequently consult him. Occasional attempts to revert to the old brutal regime were seen off and concessions, such as the right to study, were won. From the island, the city looked so, so close, as though one could almost reach out and grasp it. Rather like Alcatraz in San Francisco.

But I kind of digress a little and want to return to 1990 for a moment. I met Rose Sonto in the bar at the Paarl Hotel where I was working. Rose was always helpful in the hotel. It was March. He had asked me one Saturday to help him clean his car and I was pleased to help. Well, as I say, he helped me out in the hotel from time to time and was an excellent electrician. Cleaning his car with him was always a good way to relax and get some good stories. As we cleaned the car, his pride and joy, he told me a little about Mandela.

"Man, I drove Mandela when he was released from prison last month," said Rose. "Driving Mandela was a happy moment for me." I knew a bit about Mandela, but not a lot. Not then. Sure, I knew that he'd been in prison for a long, long time. And I knew something about South African apartheid and its resistance.

"On the day of his release, when the world was waiting to see him, we lost him in the afternoon! There were no or very few cell phones around here in those days of course. How we panicked! People were sent far and wide to seek him out. Finally, thank God, we discovered him in Rondebosch East, safe and sound. Well, we arrived at the house of activist Saleem Mowzer, where we found Mandela, who had taken off his shoes, was sitting, relaxed—sipping a cup of rooibos tea! Man, he was good to see. 'I was wondering what had happened to you two,' Mandela said, smiling."

The three of them — Mandela, Rose and Saleem, finally returned to City Hall where a 60,000-strong crowd was waiting in the fading light. "Madiba was ready to make his speech, but the microphone was lousy and he didn't have his spectacles," said Rose. "He borrowed someone's reading glasses which didn't work that well, but when he raised his right fist in salute and then, then… broke his enforced silence, well… my word… well…"

That first greeting to his followers is well-documented. Rose quoted Mandela: "I stand here before you," Mandela introduced himself to the crowd, "not as a prophet, but as a humble servant of you, the people." Rose stopped cleaning the car for a moment. "To rapturous cheers he ended by quoting his own words from the sabotage trial that sent him to jail for life." Rose cleared away the buckets and rags. He stood and looked at me. "After Mandela joined in the singing of the ANC anthem, *Nkosi Sikelel'iAfrika*, the crowd began drifting into the night and the focus turned to where he would spend his first night of freedom. Archbishop Tutu's official residence of Bishopscourt was chosen. Two days later, Mandela entered his own home in Soweto for the first time in nearly 30 years." Rose walked with me through the hotel's garage and back to the rear of the hotel.

"You know," he said. "I can remember the beginning of the speech he gave on the day of his release: 'We have waited too long for our freedom. We can no longer wait. Now is the time to intensify the struggle on all fronts. To relax our efforts now would be a mistake which generations to come will not be able to forgive. The sight of freedom looming on the horizon should encourage us to redouble our efforts. It is only through disciplined mass action that our victory can be assured. We call on our white compatriots to join us in the shaping of a new South Africa. The freedom movement is a political home for you too...'"

THE TUNNEL:

DEATH OF
PRINCESS DIANA

One of the oldest and most important institutions in France is L'Académie française, a body that exists to regulate the usage of the French language. Wonderful idea! One thing that often causes confusion is the gender of nouns. Most French people won't correct someone who says *un chose* instead of *une chose*, but they may roll their eyes a little and wince perhaps. I recall causing much hilarity when I once said *"du beurre et du confiture"* in one of our French restaurants. It was explained to me that it's *"du beurre et de la confiture"*. I don't know why my small error was so funny, but it was.

French people also always say *bonjour* and *au revoir* when they enter or leave shops, buses, meetings or even when beginning a conversation. I made the mistake of asking a taxi driver a question without first saying *bonjour*. Needless to say, he was less than impressed. And formality is even more important in written French. When French people sign letters, they don't just give it a half-hearted "Sincerely". Instead, you get something along the lines of *"Veuillez agréer, Madame, l'expression de mes sentiments les meilleurs."* It's a bit of a mouthful, but it's polite and that's what counts.

To the French, lunch is a sacred time. It's not a hurried affair, like this, involving a quick sandwich. Would you like more? Sure, no problem… Hi Sarah, could you see if we can have some more sandwiches? Thanks… Yes, for the French, it's a much-needed opportunity to rest and recharge after having worked a gruelling three hours. Lunch generally lasts for two hours and it's useless trying to circumnavigate that allowance or interfere with its progress. If, at any point between the hours of noon and two in the afternoon you feel like being productive — or if you just want to buy a newspaper, some bus tickets or go shopping — forget it. The only businesses that are really open at this time are restaurants. Even most museums close between noon and two.

Paris is relaxed and I like that. Yes, sure, some Parisians are a bit stuffy about language and foreigners — and actually about other French people from anywhere other than Paris. But Paris really does have romance in the air. The buildings, the language, the music, the food, the wine, the rich, the famous, the drama. Do you know Pamela Harriman? She was the U.S. Ambassador to France and companion to many famous men, including Randolph Churchill, diplomat W. Averell Harriman and Fiat heir Gianni Agnelli. In February 1997, at the age of 76, she died while swimming in the pool of the Paris Ritz. I like the Ritz. It's one of those traditional, smart and elegant hotels which doesn't ever change. Coco Chanel liked it so much that she lived there permanently for over 30 years.

You'll remember Diana, Princess of Wales? Of course. I was at The Ritz in 1997, not working no, but as a guest. Diana was seeing Dodi Fayed. The hotel was owned by Dodi's father, Mohammed Al-Fayed. He owned The Ritz and Harrods department store in London. Y'know, I was always intrigued by what happened that evening. It was discovered months after the accident that security cameras at the hotel recorded an Algerian woman running a hoover over the first floor corridor carpet just before the Princess and Dodi Fayed walked along the same stretch of corridor. In court, much later, Bill McKay, a security analyst, said: "If you look closely, you can clearly see a back and forth sweeping motion." He went on to say, "Configured correctly an upright Electrolux emits a low, almost inaudible vibration which will explode the brakes of any Mercedes S-Class parked within a 500 yard radius." Wow, hey? Unlikely I'd say! I'm not big on conspiracy theories, but the whole episode is a very odd one and we may never know the truth of what happened.

Well, Diana and Dodi were staying at the hotel at the same time as I, but heavy security wasn't particularly evident. If it was there, it was subtle. But these guys were hot news. I mean, really hot. That particular evening, Diana and Dodi exited through a

back door, but it was a poor getaway and the departure became a high-speed car chase away from the paparazzi. Y'see, one decent photo of Diana and Dodi could have fetched hundreds of thousands of dollars from magazines. Well, it all ended so tragically in that fatal car crash. Within minutes two ambulances reached the accident spot, but it took almost an hour to get the people out of the damaged car. At half past one in the morning, Diana was admitted to La Pitié-Salpêtrière Hospital. She died there. Doctors were of the opinion that she could have been saved if she had been brought to the hospital earlier. Dodi and driver Henri Paul were both pronounced dead at the scene. Bodyguard Trevor Rees-Jones was badly injured, but survived.

Officially, the cause of the crash is attributed to the driver Henri Paul. The official findings stated that he was driving that night while drunk. In an effort to elude pursuing paparazzi, he lost control of the vehicle in the Pont de l'Alma road tunnel. He was more than three times over the legal blood-alcohol limit and, if I knew that I was going to be driven by someone in that condition, I wouldn't get into the car. Neither, I hope, would you.

No one could attract attention to an issue like Diana. She understood the importance of a well-timed gesture and this, combined with her natural impulse to reach out to the most marginalised in society, led to one of her most memorable acts. In April 1987, when ignorance about HIV and AIDS was still rife, Diana shook hands with an HIV-positive patient. The photograph made front-page news around the world. Diana made philanthropy appetizing. She paved the way for other celebrities to do the same. Her legacy might be mixed, but it's not zero.

AND IN THE END:

THE HANDOVER OF
HONG KONG

I was working in Hong Kong — loved it. The way of life, the food, the hustle, the bustle, the drama. As you fly in, it looks as if the city was dropped from a great height perfectly formed and neat into a large crater between the hills and the sea. I had been asked to meet the official party at Government House and to escort the top brass with some of my team to the hotel. Chris Patten and his family along with senior people were moving out of government house and, officially anyway, they had to leave on June 30, 1997, the day of the handover to China.

I was given a briefing by two of Chris Patten's team because the hotel was being used by many of the dignitaries attending — and also because there were a number of lunches and dinners to be organised for the coming week. I sat with the two civil servants, both quite formal in manner and dress. I was with two of my team. Civil servant number one began counting items off on his fingers in-between jabbing at a map, "The public will be treated to a fireworks display over Victoria Harbour. Crowds of tourists and locals will turn out in the harbour area to admire the fireworks while the media begin interviewing people for their thoughts about the handover and the future of Hong Kong." I wondered what he would have done had he run out of fingers.

The second civil servant took a gulp of his whisky and soda — obviously allowed on duty — and continued, "Well now, the Handover Ceremony will begin with the British and Chinese representatives giving speeches leading to the formal handover at midnight. The British flag will be lowered for the last time at the stroke of midnight. Police all over Hong Kong will have changed their colonial insignia to a new one representing Hong Kong as the Special Administrative Region (SAR) of the People's Republic of China. Governor Patten will step down as the last Governor of Hong Kong and Mr. Tung Chee Hwa will became the first Chief Executive of Hong Kong SAR. Hong Kong will cease to be a British Colony." He looked around with an air of finality and some satisfaction, not I think because of the forthcoming occasion and not really because he was pleased with what was about to happen, but because he was discharging his duties. The briefing went on and on and the details became, well, more detailed. Afterwards, I took a walk around the city. Entrepreneurs were busy at work.

Hong Kong is like that, I think. Almost all businesses in Hong Kong were offering some sort of Handover-related souvenirs. Popular examples included Handover T-shirts, watches, bags, toys, candy. Perhaps the most interesting souvenir was a tin of "Canned Colonial Air" advertised as "The Last Gasp of an Empire".

The Hong Kong Tourist Association had promoted the Handover as a historical event to tourists and launched a "100 days of wonders" campaign. I recall that a certificate was offered to tourists for visiting Hong Kong during this period. Hotel rates rose dramatically as we anticipated large numbers of incoming tourists. This made perfect sense since the Handover Ceremony had a public dimension as well. Good for business certainly. And why not?

The Hong Kong Handover marked the end of British Imperialism in Asia and was an excellent opportunity for both

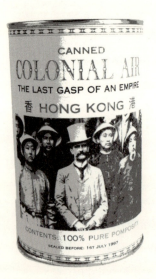

sides to close an unfortunate chapter in history that was driven by gunboat diplomacy and by the sale of opium. Unfortunately, Prince Charles, heir to the British throne, who attended the Handover ceremony, apparently described the Chinese leaders at the ceremony as "appalling old waxworks" among other things in his journal entry titled *The Handover of Hong Kong or the Great Chinese Takeaway*. Eight years later, this journal was published in the UK. It was published without his permission and I think he sued. But the damage of course was done.

As planned, the Handover of Hong Kong from its rulers of 150 years to the Chinese took place at midnight on July 1, 1997. The ceremony was accompanied by the sort of pomp and grand symbolism expected of an aging empire giving up its last great possession. The day itself had been rain-filled and grey. The clouds were low and everything was damp and dismal. I'd been invited to join the formal party — which was a genuine honour indeed. The Handover Ceremony was held in the new Hong Kong Convention and Exhibition Centre. British and Chinese delegations along with the media had arrived in Hong Kong to attend the ceremony. The British delegation included Prince Charles, Prime Minister Tony Blair, Foreign Secretary Robin Cook and, of course, Chris Patten. The People's Republic of China was represented by President Jiang Zemin, Prime Minister Li Peng and Foreign Minister Qian Qichen. Tens of thousands partied, hundreds of fireworks exploded and the flags even had an artificial breeze to flutter it. It was really sad to see Chris Patten cry as the Union Jack was pulled down and the PRC flag went up. The BBC report said the skies were crying for Hong Kong. Hmm. The Chinese reports said the rain had come to wash away the last vestiges of colonialism from the land. Double hmm.

It was a bizarre mix of drenched people: millions of Chinese who just wanted to see the fireworks and Japanese tourists taking photos of the British police officers, wrongly believing it must be their last day of work. 25,000 fireworks lit up the sky in just 20 minutes, made all the more surreal as each explosion sparkled through the pouring rain. The display ended with a huge bang as the deafening noise of six titanium maroons echoed around the Hong Kong skyscrapers. Then all of a sudden, everything was quiet, apart from the sound of cheers and applause floating across the harbour. After midnight, there came a deafening salute from all the ships around the harbour, and the fire ships spouted great arcs of water.

Alone, although surrounded by many, many people, I watched the distant lights of the British Empire travel towards the horizon. I saw one of the briefing gentlemen, the still smartly dressed civil servant, at the party afterwards at our hotel. As he turned to go in search of colleagues, he thanked me — and my staff — for our support and said softly but without looking me in the eye, "You know, the fireworks were not for us, the smiles on the Chinese faces were not for us, the celebration was not for us. All we had were some tears and not a little sadness. *That* was for us. Goodnight, sir, and once again, many thanks."

THE KILLING FIELDS:

POL POT'S BRUTAL
REGIME AND ITS END

"Hello, excuse," said the very frightened man pushing a sealed white envelope into my hands. "I have small time. You give. Man in room 1613. Thank you. Please you. I beg you, please make sure he gets. One six one three." And the frightened man bowed and walked in quick but small steps out of the foyer.

Well, the gentleman in room 1613 never did receive the letter. He had left that very day — no forwarding address, nothing. He was from France and that was all I knew — and his name was... well that doesn't matter now.

Siem Reap is the capital city of a province of the same name in northwestern Cambodia, and a popular resort town as the gateway to the Angkor region. You've never been there. But you should, maybe one day. Located in the heart of the city, in the Old French Quarter only eight or so miles from the extraordinary Angkor Wat temple complex, was the Raffles Grand Hotel d'Angkor, the ideal place from which to explore the area. The sunsets over Tonle Sap Lake are spectacular. Plus that's where I rode an elephant.

Later, many years later, I discovered that the man who had wanted me to deliver the white envelope to room 1613 was the son of one of Saloth Sar's classmates. Saloth Sar and the envelope man's father both studied radio electronics at the Engineering School of Information and Digital Technologies in Paris from 1949 to 1953. Now, the hotel's policy was to keep any letters with no forwarding address for 12 months and then dispose of them. However, for some reason this letter was forwarded to me because my name was on the front of the envelope as the person who had been asked to give the letter to its intended recipient. Also on the envelope had been written *privé et confidentiel*. I only read the letter's contents because the seal had become unstuck and it had been opened already. I have it here. Let me read it to you. It's written in French and was dated 1998. The translation's not bad.

"My dear Saloth Sar,

"Although I understand that you are now known as Pol Pot. Either way, I wish you greetings. My father also sends his… regards. He remembers you well too but not, I fear, so fondly as I.

"I wanted to let you know that I have been promoted in my government post! I'm now one of the new leading electronic scientists and we have a major job for the military which of course I can't discuss. But I am coming to Cambodia and I thought that we might meet. What do you think about that?

"It's been a long time, my friend. And I know that you are unwell. And so much has happened since we last met all those years ago. Of course, I had heard about you and what you were up to. What a change from the quiet, gentle student I knew! I heard that the underground communist party secretary, Tou Samouth, had been arrested and later killed while in custody. You had often said that he was a kind man. I also heard that you had become the acting leader of the party. And then elected secretary of the party's central committee. I know that you've been in hiding after your name was published in a list of leftist suspects. I'm told you fled to the Vietnamese border region and made contact with Vietnamese units fighting against South Vietnam.

"I know you convinced the Vietnamese to help the Cambodian socialists set up their own base camp. My brother told me these things... The party's central committee met and issued a declaration calling for armed struggle, a struggle to the death. I read that in the border camps, the ideology of the Khmer Rouge was gradually developed. You broke with Marxism and declared that rural peasant farmers were the true working class proletarian and lifeblood of the revolution. Many teachers and students left the cities for the countryside to join the movement. From France too. My brother — he was one. My sister... I want to talk to you about these two people.

"I cannot imagine how you, the gentle Sar, Mr. Pol Pot, formed such a violent armed resistance movement, a movement that became known as the Khmer Rouge. You waged a guerrilla war against the government. And the people.

"I'm told that you have malaria now. But I know you'll be here in Siem Reap at the same time as me, although I think that we won't meet. I wanted to meet you. I wanted to meet the man, my old friend, who conducted a rule of terror that led to the deaths of nearly a quarter of Cambodia's seven million people — by the most widely accepted estimates — through execution, torture, starvation and disease. I wanted to meet that man.

"They say that you and your Khmer Rouge tore apart Cambodia in an attempt to 'purify' the country's agrarian society and turn people into revolutionary worker-peasants. You emptied the cities, pulled families apart, abolished religion and closed schools. Everyone was ordered to work, even children. Your Khmer Rouge outlawed money and closed all markets. Doctors were killed, lawyers too and teachers — as were most people with skills and education who threatened the regime.

"And you! You persecuted members of minority ethnic groups — the Chinese, Muslim Chams, Vietnamese and Thais who had lived for generations in the country and any other foreigners — in an attempt to make one pure Cambodia. Non-Cambodians were forbidden to speak their native languages — or to exhibit any foreign traits. Even French. And you ordered the assassination of a political associate. You blamed Son Sen for his fading grip on the movement. You not only ordered Son Sen to be killed, but also told followers to execute more than a dozen of his relatives, including his grandchildren.

"I do hope you receive this letter and, if we don't meet, please remember me as we were. There was little evident in the time that we were together in Paris that suggested any future... hatred. I only knew you as warm.

"For what you did to my family and my people, *j'espère que vous pourrir dans l'enfer. J'espère que vous pourrir dans l'enfer.*"

Well, Poll Pot — whatever the world's views of what he did — he was arrested by Khmer Rouge military Chief Ta Mok in June 1997. He hadn't been seen in public since 1980, two years after he was overthrown by an invading Vietnamese army. He was sentenced to death in absentia by a Phnom Penh court soon afterwards. In July, he was subjected to a show trial for the death of Son Sen and sentenced to lifelong house arrest. He died of heart failure, according to his Cambodian jailers. He was 73 years old. It's rumoured that he was poisoned.

The letter? Well, the letter was dated April 13, 1997. Pol Pot died on April 15, 1998. This is it. Before I received it someone wrote this on the envelope, which as I said had been opened: "An estimated one and a half million people living in Cambodia were killed during the brutal regime of Pol Pot and the Khmer Rouge. Their bodies were buried in mass graves that became known as the killing fields."

REACHING
FOR THE SKIES:

THE PETRONAS
TWIN TOWERS

I was at the InterContinental on Jalan Ampang, having coffee with an old colleague, someone who'd retired and was regaling me with his stories about children and grandchildren. I confess that I was becoming a bit bored. But then he began talking about his eldest son, a highly awarded architect — and the buildings on which he'd been working. I often become a little saddened by some of the world's architecture. Some are fabulous and some certainly are not, not by any stretch. I have often watched the building of the horrible new and the destruction of the beautiful old.

Jeddah's Kingdom Tower is set to become the world's tallest building, but who knows? It's interesting how tall buildings are measured. That's something of a science, but not an exact one. My coffee partner told me that in 1996, as a response to the dispute as to whether the Petronas Towers in KL or the Sears Tower in the States was taller, buildings were ranked in four categories, none of them particularly helpful. For instance, spires are considered integral parts of the architectural design of buildings, whereas antennae may be added or removed at will or whim. The Petronas Towers, with their spires, are thus ranked higher than the Sears Tower (now called the Willis Tower) with its antennae, despite the Petronas Towers' lower roofs and lower highest point. Confusing, hey?

Until 1996, the world's tallest building was defined by the height to the top of the tallest architectural element including spires, but not antennae. This led to a rivalry between the Bank of Manhattan Trust Building and the Chrysler Building. The Bank of Manhattan Trust Building had only a short spire and was 927 feet (or I think it's 283 metres) tall and had a much higher top occupied floor (the second category in the 1996 criteria for tallest buildings). By contrast, the Chrysler Building had a very large 125 feet spire *secretly* assembled inside the building, only deployed at the end of its construction, to claim the title of world's tallest building with a total height of 1,048 feet — although it had a lower top occupied floor and a shorter height when both buildings' spires were excluded. Still confusing, ain't it?

Apparently, upset by Chrysler's victory, Shreve & Lamb, the consulting architects of the Bank of Manhattan Trust Building, wrote a newspaper article claiming that their building was actually the tallest, since it contained the world's highest usable floor. Good point, I think. Anyway, who cares? Well, they did. They pointed out that the observation deck in the Bank of Manhattan Trust Building was nearly 100 feet above the top floor in the Chrysler Building, whose surpassing spire was strictly ornamental and inaccessible. At present, the Burj Khalifa tops the list by some margin, regardless of which criterion is applied. The 2,717 feet tall Burj Khalifa in Dubai has been the world's tallest building since 2008.

Well now, here I was in KL being lectured on buildings. The Petronas Twin Towers were completed in June 1996 with the official opening taking place on August 31, 1999 by Mahathir Mohamad, the fourth Prime Minister of Malaysia. Most of architect César Pelli's buildings look like a postmodern future as imagined by Fritz Lang in the movie *Metropolis*. His twin Petronas Towers seem to be a mix of New York Art Deco fused with local Malaysian styles and cast in concrete and glass... You do? Yes, I like it too. You can almost imagine shimmering electrical plasma rings moving up and down the two towers. It's impressive.

In the first few years of their being, the towers were celebrated as a cultural phenomenon, even featuring in the blockbuster Hollywood movie *Entrapment*, like some giant product placement. The Towers have become an icon and symbol of Kuala Lumpur. The buildings are 88 stories high and the sky bridge between the two towers is at Level 41, with a viewing deck on level 86. The architectural design of the towers is not only distinct and striking, it also recognises Islam and Islamic geometric principles — Islam of course being the official religion of Malaysia.

The floor of each tower is based on Islamic geometric forms of two squares, each of which interlocks to create the shape of eight-pointed stars. This represents the Islamic principles of unity, harmony, stability and rationality. The pinnacles of each tower are not just for decoration. They actually house aircraft warning lights and external maintenance building equipment such as window-washing equipment. Each pinnacle features a spire with 23 segments and a ring ball comprised of 14 rings of varying diameters. The Towers feature multifaceted walls of 33,000 stainless steel panels and 55,000 glass panels. I wondered about the significance of the 88 stories and I asked this of my coffee companion who had by now ordered local cake — known as brown sugar cake or *kuih talam*. Very sweet — far too sweet for me. But he happily munched away.

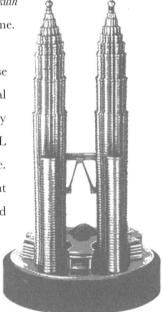

Well, he let me know that in the Chinese tradition, the number 88 means perpetual prosperity. This factor was and is very important for the Chinese people in KL who came from the Guangdong province. I advised the Chinese government on aspects of the 2008 Olympics and discovered some interesting facts about the number eight. Number 88 symbolises fortune and good luck in Chinese culture, since the word for eight (bā, 八) sounds similar to the word which means wealth in Mandarin or Cantonese (fā, 发). I discovered that in Chinese supermarkets, prices often contain many eights. The shape of the Chinese character for eight (八) further implies that a person will have a great, wide future as the character starts off narrow and gets wider toward the bottom, a bit like a narrow-waisted woman... And a license plate with an eight in it is seen to have high value and luck. The 2008 Beijing Olympics opened at eight in the evening on August 8, 2008.

The Towers are predominantly office buildings with Tower One used exclusively by Petronas (Petroliam Nasional Berhad), the State owned oil and gas company. Yes that's right — Petronas has sponsored the Mercedes Formula One team for some time. Tower Two contains office spaces for other companies and there's a big shopping mall at the bottom. I don't much care for the mall. I don't much care for any mall whether it's in New York, Dubai, London or KL. But standing at one of the high observation points in the Towers is something. If it's a clear day, not always the case, the view is something too. Seeing the orange sun sink and set, or watching the rain against the windows and the lights in the city as the sky grows dark — that too is something.

TELLING THE TIME:

THE BIG WORRY OF YEAR 2000

In offices throughout the world, at Christmas time or at the end of the year, managers are hauled before a gaggle of employees, some worse for wear, and invited to give a short speech or toast. Each year they struggle to figure out what to say. These A-type personalities typically have no problem chairing a meeting, discussing strategy, or terminating, often with cold-blooded efficiency, their faithful employees.

These captains of industry, often bedecked in reindeer sweaters, are suddenly rendered mute, unable to utter much of any welcome or sense. Instead, they wander to the speaking gallows with a pitiful mug of alcohol-free, sugar-free, gluten-free, taste-free rum punch grasped weakly in a fist, give a wan smile, mutter something about the season being a time for sharing and maybe quoting something by Dickens or an obscure philosopher. I look on these things like this. It's the holidays. For the last 51 weeks employees have been hearing nothing but planning and strategy from you. Time to loosen up a bit. Instead of opening your remarks with something banal such as "I'd like to thank all of you for being here" (not that the poor people had much choice), I like to challenge myself by saying "I want to share a story with you." You will have their full attention, I guarantee. But what story to tell? Well, it's your story. Preferably, one that is short (under a minute is best) that reveals the main idea of your remarks. If your main idea is about working together, your story should be about that. Just share a memory. An example?

OK, something like this maybe…. "When I was a young boy, my family had this tradition where we'd hop in the station wagon on Christmas Eve and drive around to look at the Christmas lights in town. We'd occasionally get out of the car and walk around. In any direction, you could smell seasonal dinners cooking. Ours was in the oven at home. We lived close by a lake and one time I remember a car in front of us spun out of control and ended up in the lake. There was a whole family inside. My father stopped our car, rushed into the water and started helping the family out. I'll never forget this next part: through their windows you could see people getting up from their tables — abandoning their Christmas dinners — and rushing outside in their coats and hats. They got into the water and everybody helped get that family out. Ladies

THE OTHER SIDE OF HISTORY

and gentlemen, since that day, Christmas for me has always meant a season for family, and a community of people, to warmly convene and work together. And that's the same spirit I find here…"

You see where I'm going with this? Why a story? It shows that you're a real person with real emotions. You're connecting on an emotional level. And then you need a little something more. Instead of the typical "I'd like to thank you for all your efforts." Dig deeper. Use real examples, mention real people and look them in the eye when saying it. Perhaps something like this:

"This year we launched our amazing XYZ pilot project. So many of you helped make this project a success: the communications team for spreading the word and helping us all understand everything, the policy team for implementing the final countdown, the operations team for making the dream come true. But there is one person I want to single out. John Doe — you went above and beyond. You worked nights, weekends, holidays. It was a huge sacrifice and I want you to know we all appreciate your work — I appreciate your work. Thank you. In fact, I want to thank all of you. It's been my pleasure and an honour to work with you all."

There's a final piece to this too. Again, nobody cares much at this moment about your strategic vision for the company (unless it's very, very brief). So, use this opportunity to spread a bit of sincere hope and optimism. Don't just say it, show it. Perhaps something like this: "I look at all of you and I feel fortunate — fortunate to work with some of the most talented people in this field. I don't want to gloss over things — we have some tough days. And just like all of you, I have my ups and downs. But look at what we've accomplished together. This isn't my success or the company's success — it's our success.

"This time of year gives us that rarest of all things: a time for reflection. It also gives us a chance to look ahead. Here's what I see ahead of us. I see a team second to none. I see a team that is prepared for all challenges and I see a team I'm proud to lead."

And finish strongly: "As my father told me, when we drove home that night after we helped those people out of the freezing water — the heater is blasting out hot air in the car, our coats are soaked with slush, our dinner is burning in the oven — he said, 'Good people just help each other out.' So, here's to being good to each other — helping each other out. Here's to enjoying our families, spending time with our friends. And when we get back next week, let's build on this spirit and help each other do even more in the upcoming year."

Y'know, my boy, Tonga is the first country in the world where the New Year actually becomes the new year. I was in Nuku'alofa, Tonga's capital, for a few weeks, meeting some of the company's board and discuss some new acquisitions. I was staying at The Waterfront Lodge, located near Queen Salote Wharf with the beautiful beach and the sea right in front. I'd had to make a speech and it had gone down pretty well, I think. It had been video-ed and sent round to all of our people.

I had some time to explore Tongatapu and a few of the other

islands. The sea views were beautiful. And I loved the Polynesian art. Still do. Look — yes, there. Like it?

Well, back then, in the bar one evening in very late December, there were few people about and I was early for a business dinner with colleagues. I sat on a bar stool and ordered a refreshing something or other. Next to me was a woman in some state of agitation. She had had several refreshing somethings or others. She started talking.

"I'm sorry, apologies — but, hi. May I discuss something with you? I'm concerned... People say it's crazy... but I do believe that the Year 2000 computer problem will be a huge for the world in just a few days' time." I must have looked surprised or confused although, in this job, over the years you have to listen to all kinds of weird stuff as well as some extraordinary things too. This chat was verging on the nonsensical. The lady looked normal enough, attractive too but that's no guide to identifying looney toons. I realised that she hadn't stopped talking. "All sorts of machines will be driven haywire by their inability to read dates in the new year: computer networks that control power, water and phone systems will freeze — everywhere; railroads, airlines and trucks will be idle as dispatch and traffic safety systems crash and the financial universe, from stock markets to payroll systems to automated teller machines, will go blank. Anything that relies on a timer or a computer just won't work." At that, she slammed the palm of her left hand hard on the bar causing several drinkers to look round and I suspect they thought that a) we were together and b) we were having a terrible argument. I made what I hoped were calming movements with my hands.

"Don't shush me," she said irritably. "Companies have spent tens of billions of dollars on computer repairs and upgrades. People I know have taken cash out of their bank accounts. I have too. People have hoarded canned food, gasoline, generators, guns… People say we're overacting, but I don't think so. Look, even the American Red Cross advises the public, as a precaution, to have enough food and other staples on hand to endure disruptions of several days to a week, to a month, maybe more. I think it'll be longer, y'know. It'll be our worst nightmare. I'm here because new year begins here. I want to be first to know what's going to happen.

"In the States, you know, The Federal Reserve has printed $50 billion in extra currency — lifting the total in circulation to $200 billion — to assure consumers that banks will have plenty of paper for those who want to have extra cash on hand before the end of the year. That means those guys are worried too. Big time. Some airlines are concerned and won't be flying over 24 hours beginning on New Year's Eve. Others say that their senior executives will be in the air as 2000 arrives. How do we know that's true? Stupid fools. Complacency leads to disaster." She stopped talking and looked down at her glass. I offered to buy her another drink, perhaps stupidly. She accepted.

"The Year 2000 computer problem," she went on when the fresh glass of green liquid with a cherry on top arrived. "The computer problem is also known as the Millennium Bug or Y2K, y'know." I nodded. She took no notice of my agreement. "After all," she said, "humans seeded the Year 2000 problem into the technology landscape by using just two digits in programming dates, such as 99 for 1999, to save expensive memory in the 1960s and 1970s. Early on, computer workers began warning that some machines and software would malfunction because they would read 00 as 1900 instead of 2000 or as no date at all. But all too human foibles like sloth, greed and unfounded optimism made them think that someone else — or new intelligent machines — would take care of the Year 2000 problem. They allowed it to grow into an expensive, potentially deadly global challenge. You may smile, sir. But listen to me... will workers have the skills and dedication to overcome whatever computer malfunctions that *do* occur? Will citizens be neighbourly, rather than selfish? Will political and business leaders step in effectively at the right moments? A minority is already investing heavily in the belief that the answer to these questions is mostly a very large no. I'm one of those. I'm not a Year 2000 alarmist, I'm not a member of a religious group that sees the computer problem as a pre-ordained divine punishment. I'm not a survivalist fleeing for a rural fortress. But I do think we're in trouble. Look, polls show that around ten percent of the world's population expect to withdraw most or all of their money from banks. A Gallup poll in December found a good proportion of Americans expected to buy either a generator or a wood stove. People do believe that electricity will be cut."

I made to move off bidding the lady goodnight. However, she grabbed my sleeve, missed and got hold of my jacket's lining. I thought it was gonna tear! "I haven't finished," she said irritably, clutching ever harder on my jacket's lining. The better part of valour bade me stay. It does sometimes, kiddo! She eased off the heavy duty clutching and looked beseechingly at me — well, at least that's what I thought she was doing.

"See," she said, "considering how much of our everyday lives is run by computers, the new year is totally expected to bring serious computer repercussions – maybe this Y2K bug is going to end civilization as we know it. Banks, traffic lights, the power grid and airports — all run by computers. What's gonna happen?" She emphasised each word with care. "What is going to happen?" She looked off through a window and God knows what dark, wretched and bleak future she saw. "Even the president," she began to wail again, "even Mr.Clinton warned — *repeatedly* warned — American companies to get ready. He said the millennium bug posed an urgent challenge to government, to businesses and to individuals in America and across the whole wide world." Here she stretched out her arms as if embracing her whole wide world. I asked if he'd actually said that. "Sure," said the woman, "Mr. Clinton said it would affect both vast corporations and the smallest businesses. He said any business which hadn't prepared would be subject to difficulties or ruin."

Well, kiddo, at this point I could see my colleagues across the bar. One waved at me and indicated that I should go join them. Boy, they weren't the most exciting guys in the world, but right then that's where I wanted to be. Yet this lady hadn't done. However, as is often the case, kid, providence stepped in when a German gentleman sidled up and said that he couldn't help overhearing what the lady had said and that he too shared her deep concerns — and couldn't he hear in full her opinions? I suspected a chat up line and it wasn't a bad move, I guess. I could have hugged him! I excused myself, wished the lady well, hoped all of our futures were gonna be OK, winked at the guy and slipped off to join my colleagues. The woman had eyes only for the new guy and didn't even notice that I'd gone, which was just fine.

INTERLUDE

Let's change tack a little… I've told you some stories, but I believe that I need to tell you something about hotels… You know, it seems to me that most hotel receptions these days are almost always staffed by women, mostly women who speak the local language — but not necessarily your own. I say this merely as an observation, nothing more. Night porters are inscrutable — sometimes helpful and sometimes not. I would hope the former is true in *our* hotels. There's a sense of mystery in many hotels. People. Rushing, strolling, waiting, happy, sad, tired, anxious, beautiful kids, plain kids, plum ugly ones, badly behaved monsters, adults, people running towards something or someone, folks running away from everything. What are their backstories, I sometimes wonder? We always wonder about that kind of thing, I think, at certain times when we are relaxed and the rest of the world isn't. When we are still and have nothing else to go to or do, but simply to watch, enjoy the watching, and to wonder about others.

I always think that hotel corridors are like streets, with identical doors on either side, paint colour beige or taupe. What the hell is taupe anyway? Grey with a tinge of pale brown, or pale brown with a touch of grey? Who knows what goes on inside those rooms — the cuckolds weeping, the lovers loving, the tired, the lonely, the money, the sex, the sleeplessness, the forgotten, the bastards, the good people...? The light in most hotel common parts is diffused and slightly dull. Yellow. Contrary to that is the fact that occasionally you walk into a reception area and are dazzled by the white bright light. That can be a jolt when you've been travelling for some time.

In general, hotel walls are covered in pictures, fixed so that they can't be stolen — which for someone like me is frustrating, not because I want to steal the pictures, but because I want to straighten them and that's really irritating when the one you want to straighten is actually fixed solid at a slight, tiny slant. The carpets muffle all sounds: heels, trollies, suitcases, voices at night, laughter and anything that rattles and rolls.

Most four- and five-star hotels have keycards for the bedrooms and, in smaller places, you get a big key with a bigger fob from the receptionist. Sometimes the fob comes in the shape of something connected with the place or the hotel's name — a gnome, a tower, a bullet, a small horseshoe, a wooden animal, a bust of someone evil or famous. I do go on about it, but in the early days of keycard technology, some room doors wouldn't open no matter how many times and how many ways you tried to swipe the thing — slowly, fast, faster, this way and that, again and again. Then, tired from travelling, you swore violently, loudly and comfortably — it was especially irritating if you had been assigned a room on a higher floor which wasn't even close to the elevator. And then, left with no choice, you trudged slowly with your luggage back to the reception desk in the hope that the second time would be better.

Occasionally, there are six- and seven-star hotels — often self-proclaimed. The understated, or maybe overstated, opulence in the design, the exterior, the interior — bring with them a unique level of luxury, even if the taste is questionable. Lavish Italian marble and gold leaf, private butler services, someone to run your bath, someone to unpack or pack your clothes — if you would so wish for such a service, I sure as hell would not — luxurious limousines with airport transfers in a Rolls Royce and a private golf cart to move you around the adjacent properties, plus a 24-carat gold plated iPad to use during your stay. But it's not what everyone wants, or can afford.

Most hotel bedrooms are more or less the same the world over — of course depending on which star allocation the place has. In your bedroom, there'll likely be a desk arrangement in some dark or light veneer, a matching chair for the desk — sometimes a very good one for your back. There'll probably be a comfy chair with a footstool to watch TV, although, invariably, the TV will be in the wrong place to view well or indeed properly from the comfy chair. So your back begins to ache again. The bed will be big, small, wide, or not so wide — with fantastic pillows or terrible plastic-filled ones. On the TV screens, there'll be a welcome message with your surname often misspelled. And sometimes your gender will be mistaken too. In one of the bedside table drawers, there'll be a Bible, usually of the Gideon variety although some places will have Bhagavad Gita, Talmud or Quran texts, depending on where in the world you are. In the drawer there may be an arrow pointing the way to Mecca.

In cheaper hotels you may find items belonging to the previous incumbent — condom packets, a half-read paperback still damp from having been read in the bath, a few biscuits perhaps, an old airline boarding pass. In smarter hotels you might find a big, shiny, red apple that looks fabulous on a small white plate with a cute fruit knife. Or there may be a bowl of fruit artistically arranged. And, depending on the time of your arrival, the fruit may be tempting or a little weary. There will be local mineral water and possibly a minibar fridge full of tiny bottles of alcohol, salted peanuts and chocolate, although again the contents of the minibar will vary depending on where you are in your travels.

At bedtime, you might come back to the room to find your pyjamas (if you wear them) neatly laid out and a chocolate mint on the pillow, which you'd better eat immediately, otherwise you'll wake up to a distressing mess all over the pillow and you'll think that you've leaked blood from some head orifice.

On the desk, there'll be one of the various styles of faux leather folders containing information about room service, making all kinds of promises — what you can do and what you can't. And when you can or can't do it. Day trips here, visitors' delights there. Sometimes this information will be dog-eared and sometimes pristine. The material may be in so many languages that you would need a full hour to find your own version. Probably there'll be a local map and some tourist information. You'll find two envelopes and one sheet of writing paper. There will be a small writing pad and a pencil or, in smarter hotels, a ballpoint pen which looks good, slim and worth keeping, but invariably won't work very well or for long. In the desk drawer there may be a sewing kit with needles that would be impossible to thread.

The TV control may have worn down so you can't read which button does what, and sometimes what you think is "vol" is actually "off". The tray with the kettle is nowhere near a socket. There's a welcome card on the tray (or near the TV set) with "Welcome to you from the management of the xyz hotel" and that too will be in a dozen languages. In your own language it will say something alarming and then amusing, such as, "English well speaking" or "In case of fire, do your utmost to alarm the hotel porter" or "Please leave your values at the front desk." Your TV will have many channels, again in a wondrous supply of languages and there may even be a couple of free porn channels. Or you may press the wrong button, watch what you think is free porn and then have an embarrassing moment at checkout when the receptionist has a loud voice, or if a business colleague is standing next to you.

There may be a safe in the wardrobe and the operation is much the same everywhere, although I always try the steps out several times before locking anything in it. Best to be safe. Yes, yes… pun intended. There may also be an ironing board folded in the wardrobe, and maybe a toweling robe or two, which will only fit comfortably if you're a size 8 model. And that causes problems when room service is at the door and you've just had a shower.

The bathroom may have a bath and a shower, or just a shower. Smarter hotels have smart showers. Some have the bath in the bedroom instead, a feature that doesn't work so well for couples who don't know each other so well. There will be two small glasses or "glasses" made of plastic and often also wrapped in plastic. There'll be a shower cap and an arrangement of unguents. Again, depending on the number of hotel stars, there will be a quantity of towels, a shower system that takes half an hour for you to work out its use and, even if you do, the thing will freeze or burn.

Decoration of hotel rooms does vary from city to city, country to country and star to star. You'll have seen that. You've stayed in enough places in your time. Sometimes they feel like a dentist's waiting room, sometimes a prostitute's boudoir. Sometimes very grey. Sometimes taupe — that colour again. Pictures are strange reproductions of gaudy flower paintings or famous buildings. Sometimes, depending on the hotel's age and its overall theme, there are a variety of artworks — along corridors and in lounges, drawing rooms, vestibules, lobbies, concierge cubby holes and occasionally in elevators — although these days there are usually advertisements for a hotel restaurant or forthcoming events which of course will exclude you because you'll be long gone. There was this one elevator in a Copenhagen hotel which had a large print of a pair of female nudes with unnecessary close-ups. It did limit elevator conversations.

Some hotel chains decorate their hotels the same the world over — with the exact same fixtures and fittings. The only differences are the languages, the accents of the guests and the views. Sometimes there are security guards placed prominently — South Africa is a case in point. Concierge personnel or those standing outside hotel receptions can sometimes wear wonderful outfits in blue with gold braid or green with red trimmings.

Air conditioning can be a haphazard affair, too cold or not working properly. Some systems won't turn off and some won't turn on. Noisy too, usually, and one always wonders if Legionnaires' disease is a real possibility. In some hotels in some cities, chambermaids will walk in to your room at any time whether there's a "Do Not Disturb" sign on the door or not. Usually these ladies are apologetic and a) carry on regardless, b) exit backwards, shutting the door softly, or c) are not ladies at all.

Some hotels accommodate conferences. Huge auditoriums ring with the sounds of tattooed crew members in baggy shorts and tight T-shirts setting up staging, lighting rigs and sound systems. There's the stale smell of ketchup, burnt rubber and sawn wood. There will often be someone dressed in pressed jeans and a bright, short-sleeved shirt clutching papers and a clipboard and not really knowing what to do, and that's the client. In the evenings, men appear wearing tuxedo suits that don't quite fit and aren't theirs anyway, with bursting shirts and florid faces. Plus black ties that are clip-on, or bow ties of any shade other than black. Occasionally there'll be a full Scottish outfit floating about. Women surreptitiously adjust their undergarments and walk in small steps on high-heeled stilettos. In the mornings at breakfast, delegates pile their plates high with fried food and eat vast quantities. Do they, I have often wondered, do that each day at home?

At a number of hotels, your bedroom phone will ring at an unearthly hour with a sweet-voiced person asking if everything is to your satisfaction. Others will have building works going on above or below you and, while you will have been warned with an apologetic note from management, it will be irritating beyond compare and will spoil sleep and affect your productivity at work. The drilling will be replaced by banging and then a pause followed by some louder bangs and then a repeat performance.

Now... *my* hotels, I like to believe, have none of these problems. Of course they don't. Well, sure they do — some. But let's get back to my stories. I think we got up to the new millennium if memory serves...

GROUND ZERO:

9/11

Well, yes... there is one September that the United States will never forget. The world too, really. I was working in New York as a manager in one of our upper market hotels and conference venues. On that day, September 11, 2001, after the second aircraft had hit, we opened our doors at three of our downtown hotels to let anyone who wanted to escape a chance to rest up, phone their relatives, take time out, have some coffee or just talk about their experiences to other frightened, anxious people whom they'd never before met.

My staff and I took everyone's details and over the ensuing months rang each and every one of those people — four hundred or so. Many corresponded and emailed us and I think lots of people did that kind of thing back then — a sort of therapy. Closing the circle a little. Some didn't respond at all and I understand that too. About six months later, I got my communications team to set up a formal online magazine so that we could share people's comments and feelings. I printed a whole lot out into an album — here take a look. Let me read out a few...

"On the far end of Rikers Island, you have a perfect view of the Manhattan skyline. On September 11, 2001, I was down there with a friend of mine and we saw that one of the twin towers was already on fire. Then, we actually watched as the second plane came in and hit the second building. On those planes and in those buildings, were regular people who were doing, thinking, daydreaming about something else when these horrendous things occurred. No warning. Just occurred. We were so frightened that we began crying."

And another, "For seven years, I was an attorney at Cahill Gordon & Reindel, a Wall Street law firm, a few blocks east of what was the World Trade Center. I live in New Jersey and my commute took me by train from Montclair to Hoboken, and then by ferry to the World Financial Center. From there I would walk to Cahill's offices and that typically meant I would cut across the plaza between the Twin Towers — usually around 9:00 a.m. And it was around that time that the airplanes struck: the North Tower first, the South Tower next, shortly after. But I was not there then. I was at home eating breakfast having woken up late, and I happened to turn on the television right when the second plane hit the South

Tower. Shocked, I ran to the television, knowing from the profile of the aircraft that it had to be a commercial airline. I have for years since thought about the 'familiar strangers' of my pre-9/11 commute, strangers whose faces I never saw again perhaps because they were victims or perhaps because their commute patterns simply changed as a result. I'll never know."

Several officers from the fire and police departments came into the hotels either to reassure people or to find out some information. They all looked exhausted and haunted. This is from one of them with whom I'm still in touch, "One of the hardest times was when people were walking around New York with posters of their family members with pictures. And we couldn't help them."

A colleague of mine left the hotel business and New York soon after. This is his story. "My wife Vicki and I were on the way to work from a near suburb — hers for business, mine for your hotel. The commuter train conductor made an announcement about the attacks and then turned his radio on loudly for all in our train car to hear. Others joined from neighbouring cars. Vicki got off to catch the next train back home. I continued on towards Manhattan to be available, to see how I might help brothers and sisters, strangers and associates. Getting to the hotel was a challenge. Out of concern for possible terrorists in the train tunnels, the conductors would not bring the commuter train any closer than 125th Street. I quickly found a bus across town to Broadway, but no buses were going south. If there were terrorists on the ground, the city did not want to assist their movement. As I waited for a taxi to hail, I witnessed a man break into a small retail store. He set off an alarm and the police arrived in a minute, while he was still collecting his loot. They weren't gentle and I was pleased. A terrible thing to think but... Perhaps the guy was hoping that all 40,000 uniformed NYPD officers were downtown helping rescue people at the burning WTC. I was disgusted and wanted to hit the man, hard. I wanted some sort of revenge. A taxicab came soon and I asked to be dropped off at a place two blocks from the hotel. The eerie 9/11 streets zipped by the cab windows and the smoke rose from lower Manhattan. I paid the cabbie and entered the raw world of NYC streets and sidewalks, now populated with quiet, pensive people. Immediately, I saw a tall African-American man in business attire, standing frozen by himself in the swirl of people on the sidewalk on Broadway, weeping uncontrollably. He and I silently hugged. Minutes transpired; they seemed to go on forever. And there were no words."

Here's an excerpt from a different mail, "At the Pentagon, I looked down and I saw a giant six-foot letter A. It was from the American Airlines plane. If you think you're going to be protected for the rest of your life from anything impacting the nation, you're just not looking at the world properly."

There's this sweet, lovely tale, "I met a guy in the street after the second plane hit. He stopped me and asked if he could talk to me. His 12-year-old disobedient daughter had made him very late. Always this daughter had been a nearly perfect angel, but that morning she had been a total pain in the butt! She couldn't find the dress she 'had to wear,' and then couldn't find the right shoes to go with the dress. And then she remembered that she had more homework to finish and she could not bear go to school without the completed assignment. He had been yelling at her all the while — and then scolding her all the way down the street as he walked her to school. Now, he's safe *only* because his daughter had thrown him way off schedule. Does God work through disobedient angels, he asked? Together we briefly thanked various deities for his daughter and her divine disobedience that morning."

Do you mind if I read some more? Here's one from a Geoff Turnbull, a naval officer who happened to be about to walk into the World Trade Centre as the first plane struck. "As many as 30,000 people who should have been in the WTC that morning didn't go — detained by a whole host of unusual factors. The WTC Twin Towers have fallen; already we know thousands have been killed, including hundreds of very brave rescuers. As I stepped out to walk along our stretch of Broadway, people stopped me, wanting to talk, express anxieties, seek answers and needing prayer."

This one's from someone who I guess was in his teens, "I was in high school in the borough of Queens at the time, quite a distance away from Lower Manhattan. I got out of class and some guy told me, 'The World Trade Center has collapsed. Terrorists went through it with planes.' How ridiculously random does that sound? I didn't believe it for one second. I remember replying something along the lines of, 'Yeah, right.' As I sat in my next class, no one talked about it. That confirmed that it was crap. However, by the following class, there was a lot of panic. Classes were dismissed early because there was chaos in the public transit system and I was fortunate to be picked up by my dad who'd driven all the way to my school. In the car, he told me to not tell anyone I'm a Muslim. I asked him, 'Why not?' He repeated the same sentence again, only with an angry voice. So I stayed quiet. We went home — and just watched updates on TV. I won't go into details on the updates — by now everyone has seen the footage. But my mom was in Manhattan. Calls weren't going through, but at one point my mom managed to reach us — and she said not to worry, that she was walking home. It was going to take a few hours, but it was the only way for her to get home. One by one, all my friends and distant friends in the area got back to me to let me know they were safe. I was very fortunate to not lose anyone from 9/11. Most everyone else I knew had a first or second degree connection to someone who went missing in the Towers and the Pentagon."

This one is a rather special note… listen, "We were 12 years old and in our first class in the morning at school when the planes hit the towers. It was the second day of seventh grade, and the only thing separating our school from the World Trade Center was a highway. I don't dream of the WTC, but I do dream of the highway."

Last one, I think, but when you have some time, do read these. I'll leave the binder on the shelf over there. Whenever you're here, read what you want. Even if I'm not around. Help yourself. "What we witnessed as we pushed through crowds and ran for our lives has become common knowledge in the past 16 or so years, though it's still fresh in my mind. The sickening thud of bodies hitting cars, the sound of the tower crumbling and our universe engulfed in the cloud. People screamed and sobbed and suffered heart attacks on the spot. We wandered around desperately for hours, trying to find a way into the east side, thinking that bombs were being dropped on the surrounding buildings, that fighter jets were shooting at us. We had no idea if we would be killed in an instant, or what was going to happen next. It seemed the world was ending. And, in a way of course, it did."

HELLO, HELLO:

THE 30TH ANNIVERSARY OF THE INVENTION OF THE CELL PHONE

April 3, 2003 marked the 30th anniversary of the first public telephone call placed on a portable cellular phone. There was a conference at one of our properties in New York. Martin Cooper, chairman, CEO and co-founder of ArrayComm, placed that call on April 3, 1973 when he was general manager of Motorola's Communications Systems Division. It was the long-anticipated incarnation of his vision for personal wireless communications that was distinct from cellular car phones.

That first call, placed to Cooper's rival at AT&T's Bell Labs from the streets of New York City, caused a fundamental technology and communications market shift toward the person and away from the place. Cooper said that, "People want to talk to other people — not a house or an office or a car. Given a choice, people will demand the freedom to communicate wherever they are, unfettered by the infamous copper wire. It is that freedom we sought to vividly demonstrate in 1973... As I walked down the street while talking on the phone, sophisticated New Yorkers gaped at the sight of someone actually moving around while making a phone call."

It's hard perhaps for you to visualise, but back in 1973 there weren't cordless telephones let alone cellular phones. Following the April 3, 1973 public showcase of a brick-like 30-ounce phone, Cooper started the 10-year process of bringing the portable cell phone to market. Motorola introduced the heavy DynaTAC phone into commercial service in 1983. At the time, each phone cost the consumer around $3,500, a huge amount of money. It took an additional seven years before there were a million subscribers in the United States. Today, there are more than seven billion mobile devices in the world. That's more pieces than people. It's not that every person in the world has a mobile device, far from it; more than half of the people in the world don't have a mobile phone, but many people have two. Did you know that over 160 billion emails are sent daily, 97% of which are spam? There are more than one billion computers in use and there are some two billion TV sets. About three million cell phones are sold every day. Since 2008, video games have outsold movie DVDs. Amazon sells more e-books than printed books. Facebook has more than 1.3 billion registered users; about 100 million of those are fake profiles. Google handles about one billion search queries a day. People view fifteen billion videos online every month. Impressed?

Well now… Martin Cooper's role in conceiving and developing the first portable cellular phone directly impacted his choice to start and lead ArrayComm, a wireless technology and systems company founded in 1992. He said recently, "People rely heavily on the Internet for their work, entertainment and communication, but these things need to be unleashed. We will look back at 2003 as the beginning of the era when the Internet became truly untethered."

Well, that power was indeed unleashed. It's absolutely staggering how deeply and extensively the mobile phone has spread, generating a connectivity and inclusivity greater than any technology past or present, improving the livelihoods of billions of people. A woman in a remote village in Bangladesh is now able to call her husband working on a construction site in the UAE to tell him that she has given birth to a little girl and that both she and the baby are well, bringing joy to all. This kind of communication has been replicated hundreds of millions of times. Of course, mobile telephony has also contributed to enhanced opportunities for increasing productivity and higher incomes. But people become so absorbed in their phones — texting, looking stuff up, watching movies, listening to music. The current phenomenon is that people become concerned if they haven't looked at their phone in sometimes just a few minutes. Look what happens as soon as a plane lands!

Now telephony plays its part in politics and the management of huge groups of people, whether it's immigrants trying to get into Europe or one person wanting to create chaos during a march in

London. These are difficult times, fraught with political dangers. Mobile phones have a huge part to play in politics and social communications. This is undoubtedly likely to grow and therefore the influence on all of our lives, in most of the world, will be more and more powerful as people find ways to change our minds, change our thinking and change our way of doing things.

In a remarkably short period of time, the Internet and mobile technology have become a part of everyday life for many in the emerging and developing world. Cell phones are almost omnipresent in most nations. People around the world are using their cell phones for a variety of purposes, especially for texting and taking pictures, while smaller numbers also use their phones to get and give political, consumer and health information. Mobile technology is also changing the way economic transactions are carried out — we can all use cell phones to make or receive payments, run businesses, order stuff, sell stocks and so on. A big use, as I say, is in the mobilization of thought, of ideas and of people. Facebook, Twitter, Instagram and all these kinds of operations allow anyone more or less anywhere to begin to shape thinking and views. As long as your mobile phone's battery is charged, you are rarely inaccessible. It's an astonishing feat.

Did you know that the Spanish, like the Italians, happily answer calls in restaurants or during business meetings. It's not regarded as rude or bad manners. Not at all. However, in Japan, a land where collective needs are put above the individual's, it's frowned upon to answer your phone in public places. Train commuters receive a barrage of recorded announcements telling them to switch their mobiles to silent or vibrate, and they refer to this as the "manner mode".

In the UK, the mobile phone is called a mobile, in the U.S. it's a cell phone, in Latin America a *celular*, in Japan a *keitai* (portable), in China a *shou ji* (hand machine), in Bangladesh a *muthophone* (phone in the palm of your hand), in Sweden a *nalle* (teddy bear) and in Israel a *Pelephone* (wonder phone). In parts of India and Africa, there is a culture of split-second calls known as flashing or beeping. Beeping is simple: a person calls a mobile telephone number and then hangs up before the mobile's owner can pick up the call. The mobile owner can then phone them back, thus picking up the tab for the call. This behaviour is practiced across Africa too. The practice has meanings ranging from "Come and pick me up", to "Hi", to "I'm thinking of you" to "Call me back". There are unwritten but deeply observed rules for flashing. When your mechanic wants to tell you your car is ready, for example, he can flash you — it's your car, after all, and if you want it back, you'd better call him. It's also hierarchical: an employee calling a superior, who makes more money, is justified in flashing — unless he really needs a favour. Not sure it works if you're trying to woo somebody!

In India, it's common for people to take calls inside a movie theatre. People don't know if the call is important, so they just pick up. Another quirk about India is that the caller may get to hear a Bollywood song, chosen by the subscriber instead of a ringing tone. Known as caller tunes, the subscriber is charged for this on a monthly basis and it's a big money-spinner. This is also common in parts of Africa where a caller might hear a quote from the Bible. These societies have a long tradition for tolerance, including allowing others to infringe on what those in the West would consider one's personal space. Some societies are more communal than ours which, in part, leads to an increased importance of constantly staying in touch.

Texting is now the biggest use of cell phones anywhere. And it's this feature that can quickly mobilise a group — small or large. It's how people gather and spread news, both the good and the disastrous. Interesting times. The power and clumsiness of various states in the world never fails to scare me — and the courage and intensity of the people in the streets continues to inspire. Something is different about political participation in these early years of the 21st century. In part, we are seeing the impact of technology on political processes.

The power of mass images is not a new thing. In the 1960s, images of wealth in Europe and the States exposed the weakness of the communist regime running the old Soviet bloc. And there was that famous video of the tank guy in Tiananmen Square 20 years ago, literally placing his body in the path of the tanks — the machines of the state. The transformative power of the mass media has changed governance and

THE OTHER SIDE OF HISTORY

made it more difficult for the state to wall off the outside world. Instead of a handful of news photographers hiding to capture images at Tiananmen Square, we now see millions of people in the street, cell phones in hand, taking increasingly high quality videos and photos of anything and everything. In the book *1984*, George Orwell prophesised that Big Brother would watch over us. It is said that if you have a cell phone, the authorities can and do know exactly where you are. Exactly.

As I say, there are billions of cell phones in use throughout the world and many of them can capture and transmit images. When coupled with social networking websites, they make millions of people both producers and consumers of information. While the information on the web is difficult to verify and easy to manipulate, it's a fact of modern political and social life that they exist in abundance.

In American elections — and Obama's in particular — huge numbers of people pledged millions of dollars in donations online. The average online donation was $80 and the average Obama donor gave more than once. In this way, half a billion dollars were raised! When the United States Supreme Court ruled that political campaign contributions were a form of speech that could not be limited, our ability to regulate the role of money in politics was effectively ended. The impact of technology on political communication is not a new phenomenon. Obama, like Jack Kennedy before him, managed to master a new technology before any other politician. FDR set the pattern when he learned to use the radio to communicate directly with the public during his fireside radio chats throughout the Depression and the Second World War.

The Internet allows people to quickly spread ideas, information and organise political protest. Information comes *to* the public and *from* the public as well. Efforts to jam and shut down these technologies are nearly always overcome by hackers and clever political organisers. Bearing witness to this is a privilege and I wonder what will occur next.

"ON SUCH A FULL SEA ARE WE NOW AFLOAT"

A TSUNAMI

I was working in Thailand as part of my various overseas postings, this time at the Duangjitt Resort near Patong Beach on the island of Phuket. I was having a great time — until the day after Christmas day.

The hotel wasn't quite on the Indian Ocean beachfront, but close enough, with great views from many of the bedrooms and all of the restaurants. It was a busy time, end of year being high season and all the hotels in the region were totally full. Flowers were blooming, the scent of jasmine was strong in the air, the skies were blue and there was a lot of laughter.

It was my day off on the 26th and I confess that I did miss being with my family back in New York for the holidays, but that was par for the course. Do I regret that now? Well, I've always said that one shouldn't wish for what can't be changed, but I do confess then — and also now — missing spending more time with family. That day, I had the luxury of sleeping in a little, or reading and listening to the bustle outside. The warm air and the gently blowing toile curtains were relaxing and comforting. Suddenly my bed started shaking — not much certainly, but definitely a wobble — and I immediately thought it must be an earthquake. They do happen in this part of the world from time to time and the occasional tremor wasn't unheard of. But the region wasn't known for major quakes and I just assumed that the gentle shaking would stop in a moment or two. I couldn't hear any hubbub, so I imagined that all was well.

I thought I'd have breakfast in the staff canteen, chat to a few people about the day ahead and the anticipated new influx of guests — and then take my Vespa off for a ride, followed by a beachside walk away from the madding crowds. I did a little drawing and some painting in those days — I still do the odd thing, that's one of mine over there — no, no comment necessary — it's to remind myself of somebody that I keep that there... Right... Anyway, I always found my scooter and a bit of sketching therapeutic and the seascapes were absolutely lovely. Beautiful.

Suddenly my whole room started shaking, not just the bed this time, and there was what sounded like a huge explosion. I looked out of the bedroom window to see a rolling black mass of water not coming towards the hotel, but going by alongside it, as if we were a ship cutting incredibly fast through a thick, black sea. There were more distant explosions to the north, which sounded like canon fire. I can't really explain the noise in any other way. Very loud cannon fire. I later discovered that the sounds were of the tsunami wave crashing into buildings cracking them open like eggshells.

The black water was billowing past — and, horrifically, was getting higher by the second. I was on the 12th floor and I was just glued to the spot. There were cars and boats, roofs and trees being barrelled along as if they weighed nothing. Look, have you been to Istanbul? Well, the river there, the Bosphorus, is dark and deep. It's also wide. This was like a raging, angry Bosphorus — just feet away from where I stood. Also, here's another image. In Sydney Harbour, or just outside it, depending on the weather you can see rolling, softly rolling, huge waves, smooth water, dark and quiet. That's what this was like. The Sydney rollers are vast but these were simply massive.

I realised that this must be a big tsunami. I heard some shouting and screaming, but the noise from the huge volume of water covered almost everything else. I saw people in the water, some strangely rigid with arms and legs moving slowly. I felt the hotel shift slightly and cracks appeared in the ceiling. Someone was banging on my door. I tried to open it, but it was stuck. We had a yelled conversation because the noise from the rushing water was like 20 trains or a huge aircraft next to my ears. I eventually managed to get the door open — and you have to know that while everything seemed to take a long time, well, in truth, this was all mere seconds. I saw a young colleague, a Thai woman, with cuts on her arms and face. She was terrified and crying. I may have been doing the same too. I was certainly terrified.

We ran from the floor we were on and dashed up the stairs to the next floor. There were people sitting on the stairs, some in bathing costumes and all rigid with shock. There was a TV on in one of the bedrooms with the volume on high — and, while I couldn't understand the language, I understood enough and I could see some of the pictures of what was happening.

Someone shouted that there were people still on the ground floor of the hotel lobby, and they were partly submerged in water, hanging on to pieces of heavy furniture or balustrades. I'm not a hero by any stretch of imagination, but I decided to go down with two German guys to see if we could help. There was mud and a huge amount of slime on the stairs, so moving around was treacherous. On the third floor stairway, there were lawn chairs and pool recliners as well as general detritus. The mud sucked at my sandals. The sound of the water seemed to lessen, but I could see through gaps in the stairway that below, whole buildings seemed to be sliding by. There were the continuous sounds of two car horns one of which diminished as the vehicle presumably became submerged.

There was a narrow gap between our hotel and the next. The gap was filled with a tangle of debris. There were people stuck in the debris. Everyone I saw had wounds of some kind, many seemingly serious. Everywhere in my hotel there were torn pipes, balconies

THE OTHER SIDE OF HISTORY

hanging as if by a string. There were baths, bedroom fittings, beds, clothes, holiday things — all strewn all over the place. And a terrible smell of sewage pervaded everywhere.

The epicentre of the earthquake that generated the great Indian Ocean tsunami was near the west coast of the Indonesian island of Sumatra. It was estimated to have released the energy of 23,000 Hiroshima-type atomic bombs, according to the U.S. Geological Survey, where a friend of mine then worked. Giant forces that had been building up deep below the seafloor for hundreds of years were released suddenly on December 26, violently shaking the ground and unleashing a series of killer waves that moved across the Indian Ocean like a speeding jet. The Earth crust's rupture was about 600 miles long and, it's thought, around 30 feet wide and three or four feet vertically. That may not sound a lot, but trillions of rock moved along hundreds of miles caused the planet to shudder. Literally. I'm telling you this because I am always hugely awed by nature's power.

Several of my colleagues told me that a tsunami can be less than 30 centimetres in height on the surface of the open ocean, which is why they aren't noticed by sailors. But the powerful pulse of energy travels rapidly through the ocean at huge speeds. Huge. Once a tsunami reaches shallow water near the coast it slows down. The top of the wave moves faster than the bottom, making the sea rise dramatically. And suddenly. The Indian Ocean tsunami caused waves as high as 150 feet in some places. Think about that for a moment.

SPEAK LIKE A PRESIDENT:

OBAMA'S ELECTION NIGHT SPEECH

Room 1120, Hyatt Hotel in Chicago. My task as a chain director was to greet Senator Obama. We had met before and this time it was good to be acquainted with John Favreau, Obama's speechwriter who would eventually become the White House Director of Speechwriting. With VIPs like this, one is always briefed in advance on the do's and don'ts — mostly the don'ts — along with the detailed schedule, although I suspect that they always hold something back. On this occasion, we were told that essentially Obama wanted some peace and quiet with no interruptions.

Four years ago, Obama spent months writing the convention speech that would catapult him onto the national stage. Even though he was busy with his day job in the Illinois State Senate and was running for the U.S. Senate, he found time to note down thoughts.

Obama was a tad busier this time round and hadn't had the luxury of time. The first draft of his election night speech wasn't finished until late in the day. You know, the toughest aspect of writing a speech isn't so much the rhetoric, it's the ideas—which take time to incubate and develop. For a speech of this magnitude it's not uncommon for politicians and their staff to work on language for months, going into double-digit drafts. It's a good rule of thumb — look at executives who write something down minutes before they're due to present. Unsurprisingly, expectant audiences are invariably hugely disappointed.

Obama took a hands-on approach to his speech writing, more so than most politicians. His best writing time came late at night when he was alone, scribbling on yellow legal pads. He then logged these thoughts into his laptop, editing as he went along. This is apparently how he wrote both of his two best-selling books — *Dreams from My Father* and *The Audacity of Hope* — staying up after Michelle and his two young daughters had long gone to bed, enjoying the late night quiet. For this particular speech, Obama removed himself from the distractions at home and spent many nights in a room in the Park Hyatt Hotel in Chicago. These late-night sessions produced long, meandering texts that were then circulated to a close group of advisers, including Obama's speechwriter Jon Favreau, a young and wonderfully gifted wordsmith. On the one hand, the fact that Obama's speeches are built on principles of oratory established more than 2,000 years ago implies that the rhetorical tricks that worked then still work now. A good speech is a good speech, no matter when or where it is given. Although I would say that a good speech has to be of its moment, of its time. A 19th century speech which was entertaining and valid then might be boring as hell now. Technique only gets you so far. For oratory to be really powerful, it has to be about something that matters and it has to be the real words of the person making the speech.

The time constraint may have led Obama to sacrifice his famed rhetorical flourishes for cold, hard facts. He probably wasn't aiming for the polished, soaring language that is his hallmark touch, but rather a more nuts and bolts dissection of the choice voters face. Perhaps he wasn't aiming for a lot of high rhetoric, but much more communicating how he intended to help middle-class families live their lives. The key I guess was that he wanted to make clear the choices the American people were going to face in November.

This time around Obama needed to turn the conversation away from him — where it had lingered producing worrying poll numbers for the Democrats — and on to the issues. This speech and this election was really not about Barack Obama; it was about the American people. It was about the country, about the direction that the country had to go to get out of the ditch in which it had found itself. That's what it was about. Let me read you a little:

"Hello, Chicago. If there is anyone out there who still doubts that America is a place where all things are possible, who still

VOTE

wonders if the dream of our founders is alive in our time, who still questions the power of our democracy, tonight is your answer.

"It's the answer told by lines that stretched around schools and churches in numbers this nation has never seen, by people who waited three hours and four hours, many for the first time in their lives, because they believed that this time must be different, that their voices could be that difference. It's the answer spoken by young and old, rich and poor, Democrat and Republican, black, white, Hispanic, Asian, Native American, gay, straight, disabled and not disabled. Americans who sent a message to the world that we have never been just a collection of individuals or a collection of red states and blue states. We are, and always will be, the United States of America." Not bad, I think. Not bad at all.

THE BEAR GROWLS:

RUSSIA'S ANNEXATION OF CRIMEA

Sevastopol, or traditionally Sebastopol, is a city in the southwestern region of the Crimean Peninsula on the Black Sea. As a result of the 2014 annexation of Crimea by Russia, the city is these days administered as a federal city of the Russian Federation. The location, depth and safety of the city's harbours made the city a strategically important naval base throughout history. It has been a home to the Russian Black Sea Fleet, which is why it was considered as a city of significant military importance in Crimea, and was probably the main reason Russia wanted to keep it "safe".

Why am I telling you this? Well, I was in Kiev in 2014 and the managing director of the region's hotels and conference venues — ready and waiting for the top job, as it happens! I knew some of the president's advisors because they asked for particular conference facilities several times a year — and I was happy to help. After all, they gave us good business. Now then, days after the Ukrainian president, Viktor Yanukovich, fled the capital city of Kiev in late February, armed men took control of the Crimean Peninsula. Non-uniformed Russian soldiers established checkpoints — and equipment was set up in Simferopol and Sevastopol. After the occupation of the Crimean parliament by these troops, the Crimean leadership announced it would hold a referendum on its secession from Ukraine.

This heavily disputed referendum was followed by the annexation in mid-March. My friends were very angry and very confused. Ukraine and most of the international community refused to recognise the referendum or the annexation. On April 15, my birthday as it happens — oh of course you knew that — on that day, the Ukrainian parliament declared Crimea to be a territory temporarily occupied by Russia. Coincidentally, I had to go back to the U.S. where I had a meeting with my Board, so my knowledge of the developments only came from the news.

One of my friends, who had to flee, wrote to me. I have his email here. Look. "In Kiev, the acting president, Oleksandr Turchynov, who has been in power since president Viktor Yanukovych fled a week ago, convened a special session of the cabinet, and spoke by telephone with the U.S. secretary of state, John Kerry.

"Former world heavyweight boxing champion Vitali Klitschko, who is a leading candidate in presidential elections set for 25 May, called for parliament to convene and order a full mobilisation of the army. He also said Ukraine should consider cancelling the lease agreement with Moscow by which Russia's Black Sea fleet is stationed in the Crimean city of Sevastopol. The lease runs until 2042, and part of Russia's action has been cloaked in rhetoric about defending the base. The United Nations Security Council was due to hold an emergency session to discuss Ukraine on Saturday night. In London, William Hague said that Russia's ambassador to Britain had been summoned to the Foreign Office. The Russian decree did not limit the use of troops to Crimea, specifying only that Russian military could be deployed 'on Ukrainian territory', and the big question was (and is) how far the Kremlin wants to go. So far, Putin's statement only talks about 'protecting the interests of Russian citizens and compatriots', but there are fears that Moscow is planning a full-scale annexation of Crimea with its majority ethnic Russian population.

"You know that armed men seized the Crimean parliament on Thursday and the peninsula's airports on Friday, but claimed to be members of locally organised self-defence squads rather than Russian troops. That was bullshit. As late as Friday, that's April 15 itself, the foreign ministry was still insisting that no irregular troop movements were taking place, despite reports of thousands of Russian military personnel landing in Crimea. Putin has not spoken directly about Ukraine all week.

"Ukraine had already accused Russia of a military invasion and occupation of Crimea, and that could now become official. Michael

McFaul, the U.S. ambassador to Russia, castigated the Kremlin with a tweet: 'Russian companies and banks with business in the west will suffer as a result of reckless decision from Putin. Will they speak up?' But the parliamentary session appeared to foresee the barrage of western criticism and roundly dismissed it in advance. Senator Nikolai Ryzhkov said Russia should be prepared for the west to 'unleash their dogs on us', but should not listen: 'We are obliged to defend Crimea, we are obliged to defend the people there. They ruined Yugoslavia, Egypt, Libya, Iraq all in the name of western democracy. It's not even double standards, it's political cynicism.'

"Late on Friday night, Obama told Russia there would be 'costs' for any intervention in Ukraine. He meant 'consequences'

but actually I suppose 'costs' is a better word. Ukraine's new government includes far-right groups and one of the first laws it passed rescinded provisions for regions with large Russian-speaking populations to use Russian as a second official language. However, actual signs of violence have been limited. The Russian foreign ministry claimed on Saturday that armed men from Kiev had tried to seize the government building in the Crimean capital, Simferopol, but had been repulsed by so called self-defence units, who took casualties. On the ground, however, nobody could offer any evidence of such an attack.

"Yanukovych, who gave a press conference in the southern Russian city of Rostov on Friday at which he claimed he was still the legitimate president, has called the new government Nazis. His role is now unclear, but the Federation Council said he had approved the use of Russian troops. He fled after signing a compromise agreement with opposition leaders, in the presence of three EU foreign ministers. Russia has blasted the EU for failing to keep the opposition to its side of the bargain and says it still considers Yanukovych the legitimate president.

"Yanukovych's flight from Kiev was the culmination of three months of protest, ending with 82 people being killed in clashes with riot police. Ukraine's new government has disbanded the Berkut riot police involved in clashes with protesters, while Russia has announced it will give them Russian passports. The first of them collected passports at a Russian consulate in Crimea on Saturday. In Crimea, there were more pro-Russia rallies and the region already appeared under the control of Russian troops and pro-Russian militias, who were patrolling the airports, parliaments and roads in and out of the region.

"My dear friend, your countryman, T. S. Eliot said something about this being the way the world ends — not with a bang but a whimper. Well, I don't agree."

He was right to be cynical — my friend back there. Why? Well, in November, NATO stated that it believed Russia was deploying nuclear-capable weapons to Crimea.

Hangzhou,
September 2014

THE JEWELS OF CHINA:

ALIBABA IPO

There is an old Chinese saying that goes, "Above there is heaven, below there are Suzhou and Hangzhou." It meant that these two cities are reckoned to be the most beautiful in all of China.

Ideally positioned alongside the Qiantang River, The Azure Qiantang Hotel at Hangzhou overlooks the world's largest tidal bore. This dramatic vista combines with a premier location near the West Lake, offers access to the airport and train station, and ensures an extraordinary stay in Hangzhou, a city on China's eastern coast.

What's the big deal about Hangzhou? Well, it has beautiful parts, but like many towns and cities all over the world, it has been built up to death. I was there on a short tour of Chinese cities. The hotel industry was flourishing in this part of the world and, while we already have some properties there, we were looking at and for others. I met with many senior local and government ministers. My team had long conversations about locations and the construction process. Our choices were good but the due diligence wasn't easy.

In Hangzhou, we were in a fabulous restaurant. The service was first class, the food divine and the conversation for once was easy. We numbered, what was it, say 10 folks. Seated on my left was a senior bureaucrat who spoke excellent English. I couldn't return the language favour, but he didn't mind and we enjoyed a really good conversation. To my right was a senior contractor who had a brilliant reputation for putting up class A buildings, working from scratch to completion in months, not years. At one point, the guy to my left tapped my arm and gestured towards the other side of the room where two people were having dinner. He told me that one of the two was Jack Ma. Well, I'd heard of the guy of course and was deeply impressed by what he'd achieved. Interestingly the following evening I was at a social gathering with more business people and again Jack Ma was there, circling and chatting. I spoke to him and was even more impressed. Huge ambition, huge vision.

Jack Ma came from there, Hangzhou. You're looking puzzled. Who's he, you ask? Wait a damn moment. Picture this. The sound of 16,000 people chanting "Ali, Alibaba" filling the Yellow Dragon Stadium in Hangzhou. As the theme of the movie *The Lion King* begins to blare over the sound system, a diminutive figure rises through the stage floor. Dressed in leather and sporting a giant spiked mohawk headdress, black lipstick and a nose ring, Jack Ma begins to belt out an off-key rendition of Elton John's *Can you Feel the Love Tonight* to his adoring employees. The song is sung badly but his followers loved it and raised the roof. It's been 10 years since Ma founded Alibaba, the Internet company that made him a billionaire, and it was time to celebrate. That kind of thing was and is very Jack Ma.

Soon, it would be time to celebrate again: Alibaba, the world's most successful e-commerce company, is preparing to sell shares in a global initial public offering that is expected to be valued at well over $100 billion. In a speech in Bangkok in October 2016, Jack Ma claimed that the Alibaba Group had created more than 30 million jobs in China. Thirty million! In a meeting between him and Donald Trump at the beginning of January 2017, they discussed the creation of one million jobs in the United States. That's a big deal.

The name of the company came from the character Ali Baba from the Arabian literature *One Thousand and One Nights* because of its universal appeal. You know the story — one of your favourites, as I recall. When I met him, he told me that years before he had been in a Malaysian coffee shop and was thinking that Alibaba was a good name for an IT business. And then a waitress came along and he asked her, "Do you know about Ali Baba?" She said that she did. He asked, "What do you know about it?" and she said, "Open sesame." Then he apparently went out on to the street and found thirty people and asked them, "Do you know Ali Baba?" People from India, people from Germany, people from Japan and

China… they all knew about Ali Baba. Ali Baba and open sesame. Ali Baba was a kind, smart person and he helped the village and his mother. So… easy to spell and globally known. That was that. Alibaba, the company, was born.

One of the richest people in China, Alibaba founder and CEO Jack Ma broke records with the e-commerce company's $25 billion initial public offering on September 19, 2014 — the world's largest ever. Post-IPO, however, Alibaba's good fortune began to slip. The company's shares dropped throughout 2015 and were down 25% in November, most likely in part because of China's slowing economy and concerns that counterfeiters were using the company's platform. Ma, who has a net worth of more than $25 billion, wasn't worried, though. Alibaba remains dominant in one of the world's biggest markets and Ma said that the West's concern over China's economic slowdown was an overreaction. In raising $25 billion, Alibaba's IPO surpassed the 2010 offering from the Agricultural Bank of China which raised $22.1 billion in its debut on the Hong Kong Stock Exchange. Alibaba was able to sell more shares due to its over-allotment which allows underwriters to placate investor demand for the stock by obtaining more shares from the company at the IPO price.

Ma's philosophy was and is seemingly simple. One, think ahead. "We got successful today not because we did a great job today — we had a dream 15 years ago," he says. Two, money isn't happiness — it's a responsibility. "When I graduated, I earned $20 a month, which was fantastic," says Ma, who taught English in

China after college. "When you have one million dollars, you're a lucky person. When you have 10 million dollars, you've got trouble, a lot of headaches. When you have more than one billion dollars, or a hundred million dollars, that's a responsibility you have, it's the trust of people on you, because people believe you can spend money better than the others." Three, expect the unexpected. "Life is like a box of chocolates," he says, drawing from a line from the movie, *Forrest Gump*. "You never know what you're going to get." Four, you don't need connections to achieve success. He said, "I don't have a rich father or a powerful uncle. We only have the customers who support us." And five, to change the world, invest in youth. "The secret here is helping those who want to be successful. Help young people. Help small guys. Because small guys will be big. Young people will have the seeds you bury in their minds and when they grow up they will change the world."

Jack Ma has been a cult figure in China for years. But he captured the attention of the world because of the excitement built around the IPO, which let investors own a slice of the fastest-growing Internet market on the planet. Then Alibaba's sales exceeded those of eBay and Amazon combined and made up about two per cent of China's gross domestic product. Seventy per cent of all Chinese package deliveries came from Alibaba sales. With 700 million people using the Internet, China will soon overtake the U.S. as the world's biggest e-commerce market.

Ma is now setting his eyes on a new goal: shaking up Chinese finance. This has sent shockwaves through the staid, state-dominated financial sector and shows that his ambitions extend well beyond online retail. "In China, because of problems in water, air and food safety, in 10 or 20 years we will face a lot of health problems, like increased cancer. So that is one area where I will invest my money and time," said Ma recently. "My second focus is people's culture and education — if we don't do this, then young Chinese people will grow up with deep pockets but shallow minds."

Born in the southeastern Chinese city of Hangzhou in 1964, Ma Yun (his Chinese name) inherited a gift for showmanship from his parents, who earned their living as performers of *ping tan*, a traditional musical storytelling technique. Ma's early life cannot have been easy: traditional *ping tan* was banned during the Cultural Revolution, the catastrophic decade-long political campaign launched by Mao Zedong in 1966 in which millions were persecuted, killed or banished to remote parts of the country. As a child, Ma was bad at mathematics, but fascinated by English. As China emerged from the trauma of Maoism and began opening up to the world, he decided he would devote himself to learning the language. For nine years he got up early every morning and rode his bike to the Hangzhou Hotel, where he befriended foreign tourists and worked for free as a tour guide in order to practice English. My guys there still talk about it you know? After twice failing China's national university entrance exam he was eventually admitted to Hangzhou Teacher's Institute, where he graduated in 1988. He worked as an English teacher at a local university making $12 a month, but in 1994 he started a translation business that took him to the U.S., where he was introduced to the Internet. At the time, China's state media was not allowed even to mention its existence. After a failed attempt to start an online Chinese version of the Yellow Pages, Ma went to work for the Ministry of Foreign Trade and Economic Cooperation, where one day he was assigned to take an American visitor on a tour of the Great Wall. The visitor was Jerry Yang, co-founder of Yahoo. The meeting would turn out to be transformative for both men.

Early in 1999, Ma gathered 17 friends and founded Alibaba in his apartment in Hangzhou, giving rousing lectures that revealed his ambition, his vision and his fighting spirit. He struck a landmark deal with his old friend Mr. Yang in 2005, with Yahoo paying $1 billion for a 40 per cent stake in Alibaba and handing its China operations over to Ma to run. The rest, as they say, is history.

Ma includes a warning in much of what he says: "Our water has become undrinkable, our food inedible, our milk poisonous and

worst of all the air in our cities is so polluted that we often cannot see the sun," he wrote. "Twenty years ago, people in China were focusing on economic survival. Now, people have better living conditions and big dreams for the future. But these dreams will be hollow if we cannot see the sun."

THE STRANGER:

FORMULA ONE
NIGHT RACE

During the 2015 race, a spectator actually got on the track along the straight after Anderson Bridge, as race leaders Sebastian Vettel and Daniel Ricciardo sped by. Given that he crossed the track, the accident probability was high, but he climbed over the fencing when the safety car was deployed. Eventual race winner Vettel described the man as "crazy" in his post-race interview. The 27-year-old man was arrested by Singapore police after the incident. CCTV footage showed he had snuck in through a gap in the fencing.

Formula One racing is the ultimate test of man and machine — pushing both the car and its driver to their absolute limits in pursuit of one simple goal. Speed. Formula One racing travels across five continents and draws global television audiences in the hundreds of millions. It's the pinnacle of motor racing, attracting the best drivers, engineers and designers, with teams — many backed by multinational corporations — spending vast sums and employing the latest technology to gain a competitive edge often measured in thousandths of a second. Sounds like a commercial.

Formula One identifies a unique genre of motor racing which has a long and distinguished history. "Formula" refers to the unique set of regulations governing the cars, while "One" denotes the championship's status as the highest level of international motorsport recognised by the governing body, the Federation Internationale de l'Automobile. For us mere mortals, watching the excitement unfold on a race day is a thrill in itself. And it's a thrill that is being ever enhanced by technological and commercial developments. Given the success of Formula One racing, it's perhaps no surprise that the world's leading companies — in fields ranging from financial services, telecommunications and airlines to champagne, foods and fuels — are eager to pay to be associated with the F1 brand. Remember I talked about Petronas? With a global trademark portfolio and a strong reputation for combating misuse, the F1 brand continues to grow. With United Arab Emirates, India, Korea, Singapore and the U.S. added to the calendar in recent seasons, the world's fastest brand shows no sign of slowing in their support of F1.

Today's teams, each responsible for designing and constructing their own car, contest the constructors' championship, with each fielding two drivers who individually fight for the drivers' championship. And with the current crop of stars competing wheel-to-wheel, the world champion is unlikely to be crowned until the last event of the season. Only the world's best drivers make it into the championship — and only the very best wins. Look on the wall. See him? And him? Good huh? Nice guys too. Speed and race craft alone are not enough though. A strong technical acumen, supreme fitness and a deep understanding of the car are essential to keep 800 horsepower in check for up to two hours, at speeds of over 300 km/h and with cornering forces regularly in excess of 4G.

Well now, while the 2008 race was the inaugural night race, it was not the first Singapore Grand Prix. There was a 1961 "Year of the Orient" which kicked off a series of races in the region, headed by Johore Grand Prix in June, followed closely by Singapore Grand Prix in September. Within a few years, it has spread to Macau, Japan, Philippines, Indonesia, and within Malaysia itself, to Selangor and Penang. Back then, the Singapore races ran on the Thomson Road Circuit which had a reputation for danger because of a couple of accident-prone tight turns, the hazardous locations of monsoon drains and oil trails left by local buses. The event was discontinued in 1974 when that year's race was cancelled. The official reason cited was a concern for safety due to its perilous track — death of racers, spectators and marshals had always plagued the annual races, but it was made more prominent in light of the fatal accidents in the last two races of 1972 and

1973. But other reasons have been suggested, such as the surge of oil prices due to the Suez Crisis, the increase in traffic that made road closures of the event inconvenient, or even the government position to not want to encourage car ownership by hosting motor-racing events. I don't know, but anyway, it was cancelled.

The new race was announced in May 2007 following the agreement of a five-year deal between then Formula One Management CEO Bernie Ecclestone, Singapore entrepreneur Mr. Ong Beng Seng, and the Singapore Tourism Board. The telecommunications company SingTel would sponsor the event and also they televised the race on Channel 5 called *SingTel Grid Girls*. The official name of the event became the Formula 1

THE OTHER SIDE OF HISTORY

SingTel Singapore Grand Prix. It instantly established itself as one of the most dramatic and atmospheric races on the motor racing calendar. The first one was in 2008.

Singapore Grand Prix was also the first night-time event in Formula One history. The timing meant it could be broadcast at a convenient time for European television audiences as well as for local fans. Using public roads around the Marina Bay area, the circuit utilises powerful lighting systems to replicate daylight conditions and the most stringent safety protocols ensure driver and spectator safety. Grandstand seating and hospitality areas lining the track can accommodate more than 80,000 spectators, while a permanent pit area with deluxe paddock facilities is located adjacent to the Singapore Flyer complex.

Around 110,000 tickets were made available. The event went on to achieve a full sell-out for all of its tickets. It also hosted the famous Amber Lounge after-race party and celebrity-studded fashion show. The inaugural race proved a huge hit, with the city's famous skyline providing a truly spectacular backdrop. The race was won by Renault's Fernando Alonso. In 2014, it was announced that Singapore Airlines would sponsor the Singapore Grand Prix, starting from that year.

OK, at the hotel I was visiting in Singapore at the time — one of our top brands, but one that wasn't pulling its weight — many of the racing fraternity were staying before the 2015 race. I talked to a number of the senior technicians and drivers and the hotel staff and I were both a) in awe of the racing drivers and b) amazed at the number of people who seemed to be involved one way or another with a racing team. A big topic of conversation was the fact that forest fires continued to burn in neighbouring Indonesia. Heavy smog was a concern. Unhealthy levels forced the cancellation of other events in Singapore in the week leading up to the Grand Prix. But the authorities and the racing gurus seemed confident that the smog would lift. There was tension in the air, not only the smog. Not all the teams were with us of course, but one could sense the rivalries and could see the huddles, the whispered conversations, the hangers-on of whom there seemed to be a limitless supply. I remember wondering what that must be like — to have a steady queue of people, an unasked or asked for retinue of beautiful women or, indeed, men.

One evening, I was aware of an argument in the bar that seemed to be getting a little loud and possibly out of hand. This was most unusual. I asked the duty manager what the problem seemed to be and she wasn't sure but said that it had been going on for some time. The argument was in English and was now plainly heard throughout the bar. It seemed to be about a job that one of the two had got and the other hadn't. Just then, an older woman joined the two and angrily told them both to be quiet and leave. Her language was less than parliamentary. The two did stop, both downing their drinks and leaving the bar by separate exits, one to the garden, the other to the street. The woman stood for a moment, breathing heavily and caught my eye. She shrugged and smiled in a somewhat embarrassed way as English people sometimes do.

THE OTHER SIDE OF HISTORY

She came over. "This is your hotel, isn't it?" I said that it wasn't mine only and explained my position. "It's nice," she said. "I'm very sorry about that scene. Doesn't normally happen and, if it does, it's rarely public. Bad form." I didn't encourage further conversation, but merely said something along the lines of that it was fine and these things happened from time to time. I offered her a drink, which she refused, but seemed hesitant to leave. "These two have a history," she said referring to the two young men arguing. "One was promoted to a high level technical position with the team and the other was, well, we let him go. Both qualified, experienced people, both good technicians, both mad about the sport. One, though, had a touch of jealousy and we can't have that."

She looked at me for not so much affirmation of that fact but with a glance that defied a response. Of any sort. "The man in the bright red T-shirt, well, he's obviously upset and angry, believing that he's been usurped by the other one. It's not the case. The other one has an edge when it comes to experience and temperament." I asked what the red-shirted one would do now. "Hard to say. He really wants to drive a racing car but he can't. He also might find it difficult to join another team as a technician — the F1 world is a very small one. He'll probably get a job with a top class motor dealer — there's nothing wrong with that. He's not yet 30, so the world is his oyster, really, and we'll probably give him a decent reference." Then she bade me good night and that was that.

I had been invited by the good lady to join the team during the race and that for me was a huge treat and I had first class seats. Sebastian Vettel won pole position, ahead of Red Bull's Daniel Ricciardo in second and Vettel's Ferrari teammate Kimi Räikkönen came in third. A 27-year-old British man strolled along the side of the Esplanade Drive section of the Marina Bay Street Circuit. The spectator had jumped over the barrier on the approach to turn 13 before darting in front of Vettel as the Ferrari driver reached 180mph on lap 36. The interloper then casually wandered on the opposing side of the circuit for 53 seconds before finding a gap in the fence and leaving the track. Driver Jenson Button claimed the race intruder must have been a "nutcase". Governing body FIA said they would request a full report from Grand Prix organisers about the incident.

There has been other track invasion incidents involving members of the public. There was the one at the Chinese Grand Prix earlier that year, April I think, involving a black-jacketed fan. Then at the 2003 British Grand Prix, a man wearing a kilt ran across the track too. And a disaffected former Mercedes employee invaded the track during the 2000 race in Germany. Crazy huh? But then the world is full of crazies.

BIG GUNS:

NORTH KOREA AS
A NUCLEAR THREAT

The number one foreign policy threat that may be awaiting America is North Korea's nuclear capability and its close ties with Iran. You may well believe of course that there are a myriad of other issues that equal top ranking: Syria, Iraq, oil, relationship with China and indeed Russia, trade deficits, immigration, security and so on. You'll have a view. Sure, of course you do.

But this relationship or otherwise with North Korea is, I believe, a high-stakes game of brinkmanship, with a whole new layer of uncertainty as the U.S. administration views that part of the world with care and apprehension.

I visited Pyongyang in 2016 on a guided tour — all rather uncomfortable and I had that back of the neck, tingling feeling thinking that at any moment I was going to be taken away for some questioning but it was the only way to see the country and then, of course, you don't see much. I know little about the place, but I wanted to see it for myself. Well, I know what I have read and seen on TV, of course, but that's not much and most of it is negative. A secret society in many, many ways. Korea International Travel Company (KITC) was my tour guide company. Photography and talking with local people was possible, but not much. Any disrespect against the North Korean nation, its leaders and its symbols are regarded as very offensive. The tolerance level for disruptive behaviour is pretty much zero. U.S. citizens have been subject to arrest and detention for seemingly minor things and it's not unknown for Americans who've been on organised tours to be detained as well.

After Pyongyang, I was to go indirectly to the beautiful island of Jeju. You've heard of Jeju? No? Well, it's beautiful and relaxing and I needed some of that. In recent years, Jeju province has become a popular destination for Chinese tourists and commercial developers. Maybe too many of the latter. The Chinese are enticed to travel to Jeju for a number of reasons, including the island's close proximity to China (about a two-hour flight from Beijing). I believe that Jeju has a policy of allowing foreigners to travel to Jeju without a visa and Chinese condominium owners are given permanent resident status.

Some Jeju people are worried that their island home is being invaded and some still recall the Japanese invasion years ago.

Another worry is that China has recently upscaled its military presence in the East and South China Seas. Add to that the fact that South Korea and China are growing closer commercially, there's a fair amount of tension below the calm surface.

After my little tour in North Korea I was keen to talk about my views with people who really know their stuff. I was staying at The Shilla Jeju. The property overlooks the Pacific Ocean, and enjoys one of the most spectacular settings. It's in the middle of a lovely, private 21-acre cliff-top garden.

I was meeting some ex-military people who have advised our business over the years on security matters. You will know, of course, of some of the reasonably recent occurrences in Belgium, France and other parts of the world that were hit hard by terrorist activities. Well, any organization with as extensive a footprint as ours has to be careful. The resort normally attracts world-class conferences and my friends were attending one such there. But this particular evening was relatively quiet and we sat undisturbed looking over magnificent sea views that I so love. So we talked, the four of us, about the world, as one does.

Well, according to them, the United States and South Korea remain on high alert after receiving reports that North Korea will test-fire more intermediate-range ballistic missiles. These tests are supposed to be a warning that Pyongyang will not give up its nuclear and missile development programmes. Without baffling you with any military science, the Musudan or BM-35 missile has an estimated range of 3,500 kilometres, which is enough to allow it to target the U.S. Pacific territory of Guam, an island with key strategic assets for U.S. forces. Though Western security analysts know very little for certain, the arms-control experts and North Korea watchers can agree on one thing: for the past two decades, a small group of Iranian scientists and military officers has always gathered in North Korea to witness the missile demonstrations.

The military relationship between the two countries no longer receives the attention it did when Iran — with its economy on the mend after years of devastating sanctions — could offer monetary assistance to North Korea in exchange for weaponry. This past cooperation and still ongoing relationship may be pulled back into focus as Washington tries to manage a tenuous rapprochement with Tehran. But, at the same time, North Korea is pushing up its nuclear and ballistic missile provocations.

Security ties between North Korea and Iran reach back at least as far as the Iran-Iraq war in the 1980s, when the two countries actively exchanged know-how. North Korea supplied Iran with hundreds of Soviet-designed Scud ballistic missiles. Iran renamed them Scuds Shahab, and its engineers began tinkering with the technology under an indigenous technology programme. North Korea also supplied Iran with its own medium-range No-dong missile, a scaled-up adaptation of Scud technology with an estimated range of 1,500 kilometres. Iran then developed several variants, including one with a reported range of roughly 1,900 kilometres. Pakistan also received Scud technology from North Korea around this time, renaming its missile variants Ghauri.

THE OTHER SIDE OF HISTORY

In the later 1990s, the solid ties between the various Scud-based ballistic missile technology programmes of North Korea, Pakistan and Iran become less clear. "In a historical sense," one of my drinking partners declared that evening, "the early Shahab missiles and the Ghauris in Pakistan were basically North Korean Scuds with different paint jobs — literally transferred from North Korea to those countries. Pyongyang and Tehran may share test data on a limited basis and perhaps trade conceptual ideas. But there's really no good evidence to indicate the two regimes are engaged in deep missile-related collaboration, or pursuing joint-development programmes."

As we sipped cool drinks, looking over the now cobalt sea, another of my companions said, "Little exists in the way of hard evidence suggesting that they exchange critical nuclear technologies today." This guy was by the way the director of one of the military think tanks based in California. "But given the history that they had, would it shock me that they have been secretly cooperating? No, it would not shock me."

Early in 2016, North Korea tested a new rocket engine incorporating Iranian technology. In response, the U.S. Treasury Department sanctioned individuals associated with Iran's ballistic missile programme. What this means for the future of the U.S.-Iran nuclear accord and international efforts to curb North Korea's nuclear and ballistic missile provocations is murky. And murky politics always leads to trouble. Tensions are high. It's interesting that the tensions have taken something of a backseat to more outwardly visible national security issues like the campaign against the Islamic State and Russian military provocations in Syria and Eastern Europe. In political circles and in the media, the North Korea issue is not getting the attention it perhaps should and maybe because there are no easy, ready solutions. In the world today, the terrible thing is that often there are no easy answers. But there is an abundance of smoking guns. Both Iran and North Korea are independently far enough along in their respective missile and nuclear programmes that swapping technology may not be necessary any more. North Korea is probably close to developing long-range intercontinental ballistic missile technology that could reach the United States and its nuclear programme continues to progress toward a miniaturised device capable of launching aboard land or submarine-based ballistic missiles. It has tested these so we know it's possible.

While North Korean leader Kim Jong-un's father, Kim Jong-il, proved by comparison to be a more predictable leader, the younger Kim has demonstrated a stubborn resolve to push ahead with efforts to develop a North Korean intercontinental nuclear missile capability.

North Korea's repeated violations of United Nations resolutions have led to a new international consensus on the need for stronger, more comprehensive sanctions. The UN, the European Union, the U.S. and other countries have begun to implement stronger punitive measures to enforce laws, curtail proliferation and raise the cost for Pyongyang's defiance of the international community. This new consensus was triggered by cumulative anger and frustration from repeated North Korean violations, the realization that diplomatic engagement with Pyongyang was no longer a viable solution, heightened concern over North Korea's growing nuclear and missile threats and a greater willingness to push China for more extensive sanctions. And the last one is another issue. The enhanced punitive measures are long overdue. That all of these measures could have been implemented years ago is testament to a collective lethargy to confront North Korean belligerence. The world leaders well know that to leave things alone is often a dangerous and worrying angle, but no country really dares risk conflict, particularly given North Korea's stockpile of dangerous stuff including chemicals, as of course we know from recent history.

Since Kim Jong-un came to power, Pyongyang has already conducted more than twice as many missile tests than his father Kim Jong-il did in his 17 years in office. U.S. ambassador to the UN at the time, Samantha Power, declared that all "cargo going into and coming out of North Korea will be treated as suspicious, and countries will be required to inspect it, whether it goes by air, land, or sea."

However, UN members, most notably China, have been lackadaisical in enforcing previous resolutions. Faced with a stronger international consensus for greater pressure on North Korea, the Chinese government, as well as banks and businesses, undertook a number of promising actions early in 2016. They reduced their economic interaction with North Korea, though it is unclear whether it was due to government direction or anxieties over their own exposure to sanctions. The Chinese took similar actions after each previous North Korean nuclear test, but each time it's only temporary.

It's scary. CNN reported not so long ago, "For Pyongyang to enjoy the benefits of civilization, it must live by the standards of civilization. Accepting Pyongyang's hate at face value is a first step toward credibly presenting Pyongyang with that dose of reality." And the UK's *Daily Telegraph* wrote, "It is dangerous to assume that North Korea would never really use a nuclear weapon. Although we may think that this would mean the end of the regime it is not clear whether the regime thinks this. In the strange, closed world of North Korea it is quite possible that the leadership has convinced itself that craven foreigners would not dare to counter-attack if it used a nuclear device."

New York,
November 2016

THE END OF THE AFFAIR:

HILLARY CLINTON'S CONCESSION SPEECH

The Wyndham New Yorker Hotel, Manhattan. November 9. Strange evening. Did you watch any of it? Hillary Clinton delivered a concession speech, calling on her supporters to accept the American election result, while pressing Donald Trump to hold fast to American values.

"Donald Trump is going to be our president," she said, speaking at the New Yorker Hotel. "We owe him an open mind and a chance to lead." But she said that in addition to respecting the election result, "we must defend" the values of non-discrimination, the rule of law, equality before the law and advance the values "we hold most dear". And she directly addressed female voters who had hoped to see her become the first woman to serve as president, saying, "To all the women and especially the young women, who put their faith in this campaign and in me, I want you to know that nothing has made me prouder than to be your champion... I know we have still not shattered that highest and hardest glass ceiling but I know someday someone will and hopefully sooner than we might think right now... And to all the little girls who are watching this, never doubt that you are valuable ... and deserving of every chance ... to pursue your own dreams."

Clinton spoke just four blocks from the Jacob K. Javits Convention Center, where her supporters gathered the night before, hoping to see Americans elect their first female president. The Democratic candidate said she had phoned her opponent on Tuesday night. "Last night I congratulated Donald Trump and offered to work with him on behalf of our country," she said. "I hope that he will be a president for all of our country. I'm sorry that we did not win this election for the values we all share."

When the two candidates met face to face, in three presidential debates, Trump repeatedly interrupted Clinton while she pressured him to answer accusations of sexual assault, his proposed ban on Muslim immigration and disparaging comments towards Mexicans and immigrants. In her concession speech, she alluded to Trump's campaign rhetoric, outlining the constitutional protections of freedom and equal protection to "people of all races and religions, for men and women, for immigrants, for LGBT people and people with disabilities — for everyone".

Trump told Clinton, "You're a smart, tough lady and you ran a great campaign. Thank you for calling. I respect you."

Well, now. Clinton was late to her concession speech at the New Yorker Hotel, across the street from Penn Station because she wanted time to reflect. She was closeted in a suite along with her close advisers. I don't know if Bill was there too. My people had set up a conference room for her speech and we had to cater for the journalists and the cameras. The usual thing. Awaiting her, MSNBC's cameras zoomed in on John Podesta, her campaign chair, until his face, chin in hand, filled the screen. Huma Abedin, her longtime aide, came in just before Clinton and then the room gave the heroine of the campaign a standing ovation. The applause was long and deeply felt. "A very unruly group," Clinton said. She wanted her supporters to sit down so that she could begin; she seemed on edge — not surprising, I would guess. But the people, well, they wanted to cheer her more.

The ferocity of the attachments between Clinton and her staffers has been part of the story of her campaign; at times it has made them more defensive and probably (in the case of her private e-mail server) helped to trap Clinton into some bad choices. Her concession speech suggested a reason for that intensity: she believed that she and her staff represented a movement, even if her opponents to her left and right never saw her that way. She said, "Our best days are still ahead of us." Perhaps just a little further off than she thought before...

Hey, look at the time! Sarah! The car's here? OK — good. We'll be fine. So, let's be off. I'm sure you've had enough. Heard enough. Drinks drunk and sandwiches eaten. Yep, all gone. Want something for the trip? No? Sure? Time to get off to the airport then. I hope that you haven't been bored? Too many dismal stories? Well, something to think about I reckon... Do I feel old? What a question. I do get fed up with "70 is the new 50". No one is saying 20 is the new 10. Or that 80 is the new 60. Means nothing. As a child, every very old man I knew seemed to have fought in the First World War and every younger one in the Second. I do tell people my age too quickly and wait, like a needy kid, to be told I don't look anything like that... Ha, you're very kind ... sweet thing to say — gimme a hug... but these days one starts to think about the what ifs and will there be new or indeed repeated experiences? How many more times will I see Venice? How many bowls of freshly picked strawberries and good vanilla ice-cream? How many glasses of wine? How many smiles at pretty girls and, more to the point, from pretty girls? How many long lunches with old friends? How many old friends? The abiding pleasure is that I got to go around the globe relatively easily, cheaply and safely. And healthily... these days I just want to be supple enough to put on my own socks... Got everything? OK, let's go. I'll walk down with you...

THE OTHER SIDE OF HISTORY

THE OTHER SIDE
OF HISTORY

New York

I told him that I would write. A diary, he said. Write a diary. Just thoughts, some random, some not. Whatever. There was music playing somewhere. Smetana, I think. *Die Moldau* maybe, or *Má vlast* he called it. One of his favourites. Sarah was there. "Come in," she said a little anxiously and looking drawn. "I'm so sorry," she said in a quiet voice. She gave me a small hug as if she wasn't sure whether she should or not. I went into the room and looked around. This was his place. It smelled of him and it was him. Sarah turned to leave. "He didn't want anything to be touched until you'd been here," she said softly. "And I haven't touched anything." She left shutting the door quietly.

The albums that he'd read from when we had met last were still there on the side shelves. The diaries and notebooks, everything written neatly in longhand with a fountain pen. Everything as it was. I turned to look at the photographs on the wall. And then I wept. Not just cried, but wept. Wept for the loss and for all that could have been said but had not been said. For all the mistakes I'd made and for the sadness or sorrow of all the mistakes that we all make. For all the moments when people are kind and good. For the hope that I wanted and for the stories that I'd not heard. For the sheer sense of utter loss.

Sniffling and with blurred vision, I looked at the walls and began to take on-board once more all the cities, the people, the certificates, the awards, the seas, the countries, the hotels. I noticed a picture of people standing on the stairs of some grand hotel. Everyone is in bright sunshine and everyone's grinning, not just smiling — as if someone's just told a really good joke. My grandfather is in the middle. Underneath the photograph and part of the framing, there's a quote from Philip Pullman: "We don't need a list of rights and wrongs, tables of do's and don'ts: we need books, time, and silence. 'Thou shalt not' is soon forgotten, but 'Once upon a time' lasts forever."

I see another photograph, a small one, that I'd not noticed last time I was here — a picture of him with his arm around a woman, my grandmother. She has her arm around his waist too. They're both leaning into each other, smiling, eyes sparkling. I look carefully and see that they're standing by a gate to the side of a building's entrance. I'm not sure where it is in the world or what building it is. I really couldn't recall if the picture had been there last time or not. I turned and looked at the chair behind the desk, ready to smile and ask him about the photograph and why it had been taken where it had. I saw that he wasn't there.

"History is not the story of heroes entirely. It is often the story of cruelty and injustice and shortsightedness. There are monsters. There is evil. There is betrayal. That's why people should read Shakespeare and Dickens as well as history — they will find the best, the worst, the height of noble attainment and the depths of depravity."

David McCullough,
Pulitzer Prize-winning historian

"When to the sessions of sweet silent thought

I summon up remembrance of things past,

I sigh the lack of many a thing I sought,

And with old woes new wail my dear time's waste..."

From *Sonnet 30*,
William Shakespeare

"Frodo was now safe in the Last Homely House east of the Sea. That house was, as Bilbo had long ago reported, 'a perfect house, whether you like food or sleep, or story-telling or singing, or just sitting and thinking best, or a pleasant mixture of them all.' Merely to be there was a cure for weariness, fear and sadness."

From *The Fellowship of the Ring*,
J.R.R. Tolkien

ABOUT THE AUTHOR

Simon Maier is a communications expert and has worked with corporations around the world. He uses storytelling as a consultancy tool to help senior executives and staff change their mindsets. He has maintained a lifelong interest in history and is fascinated by what goes on behind the world's big news stories. In this book, he explores what might have been the scenarios underneath what we are told. If all the world's a stage then what goes on backstage is as important as what we see.